D0197465

Femme
d'Adventure

Praise for
Femme d'Adventure

"Jessica Maxwell is funny and brave. Travelling with her is an uproarious journey to places of uncommon interest. This book gave me a serious case of wanderlust."

> — Kathleen Dean Moore, author of
> *Riverwalking: Reflections on Moving Water*

"Passion and adventure—Maxwell's got it!"

> — Yvon Chouinard, founder of
> Patagonia clothing company

"This fun, funny and insightful book is proof once again that because Jessica Maxwell exists, my feminine side need not exist. What a relief to us both. Maxwell is out there doing what historically only we male travel writers have done: touching all the far-flung, risky bases, and doing it very well indeed."

> — Randy Wayne White, author of *North of Havana*, the fifth in his Doc Ford Eco-series

Femme d'Adventure

TRAVEL TALES FROM INNER MONTANA TO OUTER MONGOLIA

Jessica Maxwell

Adventura
BOOKS
AN IMPRINT OF SEAL PRESS

Femme d'Adventure is an Adventura Book, published by Seal Press. All rights reserved. No part of this book may be reproduced in any form, except for the quotation of brief passages in reviews, without prior written permission from Seal Press. Seal Press, 3131 Western Avenue, Suite 410, Seattle, Washington 98121. sealprss@scn.org

Library of Congress Cataloging-in-Publication Data
Maxwell, Jessica
Femme d'adventure : travel tales from Inner Montana to Outer Mongolia / Jessica Maxwell.
1. Maxwell, Jessica—Journeys. 2. Voyages and travels. I. Title.
G465.M398   1997   910.4'5—dc21   97-27809
ISBN 1-878067-98-2

Printed in Canada
First printing, October 1997
10 9 8 7 6 5 4 3 2 1

Acknowledgments appear on page 236, which constitutes a continuation of the copyright page.

Distributed to the trade by Publishers Group West
In Canada: Publishers Group West Canada, Toronto
In Europe and the U.K.: Airlift Book Company, London
In Australia: Banyan Tree Book Distributors, Kent Town

Cover design by Trina Stahl
Cover photograph of Jessica Maxwell provided by Marshall Noice. Cover photographs of map and compass provided by © 1997 Photodisc, Inc.
Text design and composition by Rebecca Engrav

To my sisters, Valerie and Heather,
my original adventure partners

and

In memory of Chris Wooldridge,
who flew high always on adventurer's wings

Acknowledgments

This collection celebrates more than a decade of incorrigible story chasing for many a trusting editor. Magazine editors are a remarkable breed, able to walk through winter while reading about summer, editing fall and thinking about spring. This accounts for their somewhat dazed telephone manner, and why they tend to wear the wrong coat. The fact that they turn out monthly works of exceptional quality is one of the miracles of modern publishing, as is sending a girl adventure writer to Outer Mongolia just to catch a salmon. Or, maybe it's a hint.

At any rate, in my own career a handful of gifted, brave, authentically literary magazine editors have reigned supreme. They are, in order of appearance: Patrick McGilligan at *Playgirl*, who despite his magazine's questionable reputation was the first to let me write truly creative travel stories; Anita Leclerc, *Esquire*'s legendary executive editor, without whom the sun would not rise on New York's publishing world; Connie Bourassa-Shaw, former editor of *Islands*, who would point to a map of the world and ask me where I wanted to go; J. Kingston Pierce, who engineered my beloved "Wild Life" column in *Pacific Northwest Magazine*; Patricia Adcroft, former editor of *Omni*, who asked me to write science cover stories after hearing me read an essay on shoulder pads; Rebecca Farwell, editor of the now defunct *Discovery Channel* magazine *(TDC)*, who let me follow humpback whales from Alaska to Maui; Bruce Stutz, the inimitable former features editor of *Audubon* and current editor-in-chief of *Natural History*, who launched my first national column, "True Nature," then sent me to Mexico to see a million hawks and to France to see one dead duck; Dominique Browning, brilliant former editor of *Mirabella*, present editor of *House and Garden*, who gave me my dream lifestyle column, "The West," moments before *Mirabella* was sold out from under her, and Stacy Morrison, her associate editor who would have given that column wings; Jeff Turrentine of *Forbes' FYI*, winner of the Best Phone Manners Award; Mary McNamara, senior editor at the *Los Angeles Times Magazine*, for excellence in story sculpting; Cindi Crain, editor of *Golf and Travel*, for giving my writing skills more points than my golf skills; Sid Evans, formerly at *Sports Afield*, now at *Men's Journal*, for getting it; and Carole Jacobs, *Shape* and *Living Fit* travel editor, who would gladly meet me in the Congo to discuss Bhutan's influence on Paris fashion . . . then let me write about it for America.

Triple Bonus Miles go to Alaska Airlines's Lou Cancelmi, Vice President of Corporate Communications, Horizon Air's Dan Russo, Director of Marketing and Communications, and Sue Warner-Bean, Manager of Public Affairs, for their non-stop, round-trip, stellar support of a Western writer's quixotic travel schedule. And thanks to Kenmore Air, whose pilots introduced me to the indelible beauty of seaplanes. An Honorary Doctor of Adventure degree goes to Victor Bjornberg of Travel Montana, for patiently treating my frequent attacks of Montana Fever. Eternal gratitude to Pam and Paul Schell for their steady support of the written arts.

A hundred blown kisses to agent Mary Alice Kier, to Holly Morris, Jennie Goode and Stacy Lewis, book editors of vision and spirit, and to Lorian Hemingway, high priestess of artful adventure writing, for penning a perfect preface. An ocean liner of gratitude to my parents, Robert and Mary Meeker; sisters, Valerie Maxwell and Heather Meeker; nephew, Jesse Maxwell Wilson, my favorite adventure partner; niece, Amber Magdelena Wilson, my favorite Macarena partner; brothers-in-law, Scott Wilson and John Beal; stepmother, Zelna Maxwell; once-and-always sister-in-law, Nancy Long; beloved goddaughter, Jessica Buskirk; Soul Sisters Rande Lisle and Lauri Doyle; and Fletcher Little, river-and-spirit guide, who helps me keep both oars in the water and all arrows aimed true; and to my best friends: Vicki Adams and Tom Amorose, Pat Barry, Rich and Susie Chapple, Dottie Chase, Bonnie Duncan, Susan Ewing, Susan Hauser, June Jackson, Guido and Lee Rahr, Chic and Karen Streetman, Greg Tatman, Rick Wendland and Tillie-the-Fabulous-Sinking-Fishing corgi, without all of whom there would be no one to travel with and, God forbid, no one to come home to.

Contents

Preface

Nothing to fear but fear itself? Like most women I understand the philosophical concept, but less how to send fear running to its damp, dark closet. And I know I am not alone in this. At some forever-to-be-remembered point in the lives of all women they will lock arms with fear and dance a deadly tango. And it will not be just ordinary fear they pair with, but fear that can undo lives and lay barren the core of the self. Call it the enemy. Some women will size it up. Some will try to deny it. Some will take it dead on. And it will not be a matter of strength or weakness who is victorious, but who in its grip surrenders fastest, and in that moment of surrender glimpses the barest fragment of the thing fear fears most—faith.

A surprising number of women live the better part of their lives without ever going outside, owned, body and spirit, by an affliction known as agoraphobia—technically, a fear of open spaces—which means that you will not find these women wading a river, hang gliding or singing with the whales. And it is a tragedy that some never will. Crossing the threshold from the living room to the front door and out into a brightening day fills them not with the anticipation of adventure, but with wet-palmed horror. Of what? You pose this question to the woman who spends an ever-lengthening stream of days within a prison of rooms and she cannot tell you because somewhere along the way a small fear, a fear almost infinitesimal, has somehow bloomed into a universe of fears, and those into a crippling inability to count herself as real, as belonging to and in the world.

Enter the role model, the woman who, if she hasn't actually tamed fear, has at least sent it whimpering into the light. Women who show us, by example, *exactly* what we can do—raft a Class Five river, fish the outer reaches of Outer Mongolia, go in shameless pursuit of the Alaskan ice worm—and this simply because they have dared to venture into and chart this territory of self-doubt and have emerged—yes, bruised, yes, sometimes battered, yes, occasionally near death, but with perspective anew and an often revitalized faith.

And then there is Jessica Maxwell, my own personal role model, a woman who reminds me of Ludwig Bemelmans's fictional children's character, the irascible little red-haired French girl, Madeline. Madeline fears nothing, pokes her tongue out at the horrific, and says to the tiger in the zoo, "Pooh-pooh." Pooh-pooh, indeed. Once you read Maxwell you will see how it fits. Here is a woman who jumps, dives, flies into experience, grabbing her unruly fear by the throat, taking it along for the ride and emerging from each adventure with it purring at her feet, a familiar companion ready for the next journey.

I was first introduced to her work while slam-dancing into the eye of a hurricane some 20,000 feet above Houston while overhead compartments busted open, the plane did the greater part of a barrel role and lightning skittered and popped along the wing. Weenie that I am, I had been praying aloud in the aisle until one of the flight attendants shoved a magazine under my nose to shut me up. She had even folded the magazine back to a particular article, Jessica Maxwell's "The Panic Principle." My situation at that moment being at the very least life-threatening, I thought, Why not? You are going to die. Go ahead and read it—maybe it will help. Booze hadn't helped. Threatening to fly the plane hadn't helped. And kneeling in the aisle had only pissed people off.

So I read it, and damn if this woman didn't nail the fiber and bone of my fear while she spun the story of her own fear of flying, and she did it all with this quirky undercurrent of insane humor. As I read on I noticed not only was I laughing out loud, I was also sitting up a little straighter, my palms were dry, my head clear, and I had retrieved at least a modicum of self-respect.

And then she threw out one inescapable nugget—a statement that, ordinarily, would have undone me. Wrote Ms. Maxwell as we jolted into the storm: "When your number's up, your number's up."

Well. Yeah. Who could argue with the hyperlogical? But there was more to it than that—inherent in her acceptance of the potentially dangerous was Maxwell's belief in *faith* as a viable excuse to get out there and *live*. And as I digested this while the plane did its bumpy hula and my stomach bottomed out, there rose up in me an alarming sense of kinship with this woman, this former fearful traveler who was now free. She had examined the innards of the belly of the beast, and not only did I trust what she had to say, I *needed* to hear it.

Again and again in these lyrical, humorous stories of adventure and self-challenge, Jessica Maxwell executes her remarkable pas de deux with faith. And she does it all with a metaphorical sense so acute, so utterly original, that I found myself returning to the images, the smells, the colors long after a story was done. But, ultimately, what I come away with is the abiding knowledge that if I dare to take up my bed and walk, hike, swim, skydive, I have merely to look back over my shoulder to discover I am not alone.

Lorian Hemingway
Seattle, Washington
July 1997

Femme
d'Adventure

At Home in the Whole Wide World

Our plane was being eaten alive by a giant ice squid. The blizzard hooded the night sky, its snowflakes now fearful white tentacles streaming across our windows. We took off anyway. Juneau's rooftops vanished like a terrible magic trick. I looked around. No one else seemed nervous. But then, Alaskans don't have nerves—which is why they can live in a place with drooling grizzly bears hiding behind the rhododendrons.

Things seemed to be going fine, and I was about to berate

myself for being a real Cheechako—Alaskan for "Stupid Bear-Phobic Lower Forty-Eight Frou-Frou Head"—when our plane suddenly turned on its side and both engines died. Just like that. Kaput. Nothing. There we were, hanging in midair, and I knew we were about to crash, probably right into a cave full of sleeping grizzlies and, of course, I'd be the only human survivor, so I dug my nails into the arm of the handsome stranger sitting beside me who, naturally, was grinning. But he patted my hand and said, "Don't worry. It's just the Lemon Creek Turn."

What the !!(@$%&#! is the Lemon Creek Turn, I wanted to know.

"It's the only way to get out of Juneau when the weather's like this," he replied. "Up on one wing, cut power. They do it to miss the mountains. Juneau is the most dangerous airport in the country, but most of these Alaska Airlines pilots are former bush pilots so they're great at stuff like this. It's just part of the adventure."

Personally, I don't like the idea of messing around with engines *while* they're taking you somewhere. Especially jet engines. Bush pilot or not, cutting power while flying side-saddle in a snowstorm at 2,000 feet seems risky at best.

But that's adventure for you.

In fact, if you look up the word "adventure" in a dictionary, its meaning always includes the words "risk," "hazard," "chance" or "uncertainty." "Exciting" and "courage" are usually thrown in, too. The masculine noun "adventurer" wins extra praise for being "daring" or "bold." However, the feminine noun, "adventuress," instantly sours into "a woman who schemes to win social position, wealth, etc. by unscrupulous or questionable means." Besides being downright insulting, this definition speaks directly to an unfortunate historic bias: Real adventure ain't for girls.

But I wasn't thinking about that when our jet engines roared back on and catapulted us into the pale heart of winter. I was thinking about why my seatmate looked vaguely familiar.

"Have we met?" I asked him.

"We danced at the Grande Ball last night," he said shyly.

He meant the annual dance in Sitka to which people wear nineteenth-century costumes. It occurs during Alaska Days, an all-city gala that celebrates the day in 1867 when the United States bought Alaska from Russia, cleverly side-stepping the Tlingit Indians who already had dibs on the place. I squinted at him.

"Oh!" I cried. "You were the guy with the bearskin on your head!"

Turned out he was also a geologist who had lived in the Alaska bush for years, where he'd run into numerous slobbering specimens of *Ursus horribilis* but never had to use his gun against one and now lived on his boat from which he caught halibut so big he did have to shoot them "or they'd break your legs." He'd even put himself through college by selling muskrat pelts from animals he'd caught in nearby rivers, which explained his Fred Flintstone outfit the night before: He'd attended the Grande Ball as a turn-of-the-century trapper.

I've thought at length about the difference between that man and most people I know. Why there was a kind of natural electricity about him, an uncommon depth charge in his eyes and a bit of wildness, too. It wasn't recklessness—there was nothing adolescent about him. In fact, safety was his first priority: He told me he never went into the wilderness without his rifle, never flew in small planes during the winter and never took his boat out without leaving a "float plan" with a friend. And he always wore his seatbelt when he drove, even in Sitka, which only has fourteen miles of roads. But the thing in his eyes went beyond knowledge and wise caution. It was more like a kind of primal intelligence marked by a distinct lack of fear.

And nested within that knowingness was the near-perfect rock of faith. You don't find this in many modern men. You find it in fewer modern women. And when you do, you can be sure of one thing: These are people who abandon their homes and offices on a regular basis and go Out There where what's left of wildness still lives. These are fishermen and hunters, birdwatchers and hikers, mountaineers and kayakers and nature photographers. These are adventurers, male *and* female, the ones still bound to the land by invisible tethers, the ones who must immerse their bodies in river water, collect red earth beneath their fingernails, breathe the green air of forests, let the falling song of the Swainson's thrush wash the city noise from their ears. These are the ones who know the slap of a beaver's tail from the leap of the trout. The ones who do not confuse the aerial pirouette of the mayfly with that of the maple seed. The ones who have lain in elk beds, crossed bear paths, noted raised moose prints in melting snow, perfumed their necks with the vanilla musk of cottonwood flowers. These are also the ones who have heard unidentifiable sounds outside their tents at midnight. And followed guides with room temperature I.Q.s deep into avalanche territory. And suffered through Class Three rapids in battered driftboats during the worst storms of this century. These, too, are your travelers, the ones who want to take tea in an old Kyoto temple, dance all night to a Galway fiddle band, eat red beans and rice in some French Quarter dive, see in person the shrouded body of St. Mark that was smuggled into Venice under a passel of hams.

These things used to be the everyday litany of human experience. My, oh my, how we have conspired to dull the list. Officially we cite "no time" as the reason, but privately confess to an abject fear of wild and foreign places. Yet we are less afraid to travel in two tons of metal at seventy-five miles an hour every day than to walk a deer path at dusk or eat an unidentified fruit or sleep in a room with geckos climbing the walls.

As for true danger, I have found that early warning signals always appear on your personal radar screen, and if you faithfully follow your intuition you will be guided, literally, out of harm's way. I realize that this philosophy rests squarely on the shoulders of a deep belief in an otherworldly goodness that many "civilized" people find naive or unrealistic. But I have tested it—and been happily rewarded—so many times that I just don't question it anymore. Especially since my father blessed my sister, Valerie, and me with what we now refer to as "Our Little Miracle": Three days after he died a few years ago I was driving by myself on Vashon Island in Washington State, and looked up to see my father's face—as big as the sky above me—beaming down out of a cloudless sky. His eyes gleamed and he was grinning an inhumanly ecstatic grin, an expression beyond any earth-bound definition of happiness— and while on earth he was a man of angst, not joy. Three hours later, while driving by herself near her home in Manhattan Beach, California, where we grew up, Valerie saw the same thing: Daddy's enraptured face lighting up the sky above her. If we could have videotaped it and aired it on TV our father's face would have changed the world. It was, of course, a highly private vision surely for our eyes only, but I knew that Daddy knew that I would write about it, so he must have meant for me to. I have, and will continue to do so, if only to offer again and again absolute personal confirmation of the mysterious and sublime force that dwells at the heart of "matter," behind the endless veils of human ego and fear.

I like to think of divine goodness as being like a radio station: It's broadcasted at all times, but you have to tune to it, and there's an awful lot of static to tune out while you're at it. However, once you internalize the truth of its existence, it makes hopping on a seaplane or into a small boat or onto a backcountry ski trail or a bus filled with "foreigners" and chickens a lot less scary. The truth is, the more you tune to goodness, the more it reveals itself to you, which is really just another way to define faith in what often seems to be an indifferent universe.

On a more down-to-earth note, there is also the issue of accessibility and expense: Most jobs are urban, most modern lives are by nature rutted with routine in order to make a living. But a month of restaurant dinners will buy you a ticket to Montana; you can fly into Bozeman and be watching the Yellowstone wolves play two hours later, then return home wholly re-enchanted by the natural world.

As for this business of adventure being for men only . . . oh, moose poop! Women have been busy proving we can do anything for decades now. And I believe that personal confidence backed by physical strength leads women straight to the river. And the mountain, the forest and the deep blue sea. There are few accomplishments more gratifying in a woman's life than building her very own relationship with the whole wide world. It can produce both an exalted sense of freedom and a wonderfully reassuring sense of interconnection. It can also give her a very clear sense of who she is, undefined by her mate or her children.

And that, I believe, helps a woman have much healthier relationships with her family and her friends . . . none of which fall apart, by the way, if she takes a week or two of private adventure time for herself every once in a while. God knows the guys have proven that one for us—they've gone off on all-male hunting, fishing and golf trips as long as anyone can remember.

So, I say, "Replace co-dependence with coat dependence!"— you'll need a lot of them to handle the range of weather conditions you'll encounter as a femme d'adventure, which, in proper French, would be spelled sans the second "d." But this is an American adventure book with an American pedigree, driven hard by my father's Scottish wanderlust and delivered in a lyrical Celtic style with definite French sensibilities, the gift of my mother, whose people originally came from Bordeaux. I like to think of it as a happy hybrid, a solid yin/yang balance that represents the truly historic growth men and women have made in the last part of this dubious century. If men can learn to be good listeners, lovers and fathers, then women can learn to be at home in the world-at-large, and know what every dreaming child needs to know, which Beryl Markham, an authentic adventuress, learned while flying over Africa nearly a hundred years ago: "No horizon is so far that you cannot get above it or beyond it." In other words, the world in all its natural and cultured glory is out there waiting for each of us, if e're we dare to grab our fly rod, pack our waterproof mascara, and go.

Jessica Maxwell
McKenzie River, Oregon
May 1997

The Tao of Adventure

The
Panic
Principle

James Michener regarded the salmonberries
pressing their papaya-colored lips against
the log cabin window. Then, in a voice that
sounded a lot like when God talks to Charleton
Heston, he said: "I have survived three airplane
crashes where the plane was totally lost. In 1957 I was
in a plane that crashed in the middle of the Pacific. I must say, we
did think that was it. The pilot made a wonderful, controlled
landing into a big wave—tore the whole bottom out of the plane.
We all got into a rubber raft and floated all night in a rough sea.

After about eighteen hours we were finally picked up by a Japanese fishing boat. But," he added, waving a long hand across the air in front of him, "if you've lived the kind of life I have, something like this is bound to happen. And I certainly would never allow it to inhibit me from doing what I want to do. I fly anywhere in anything."

Both of us had flown thousands of miles to be in Sitka, Alaska, that Fourth of July weekend—Michener to celebrate the release of his book *Alaska,* me to celebrate Michener. But I would not have been there at all—would never have seen Alaska nor met Michener—had I not years earlier cured one of the most crippling cases of Fear of Flying ever to infect a ground-bound creature.

It is an elemental truth that if you elect to run around the world these days, chasing wild animals and adventure, you have to be on very stable footing with airplanes. Now, many highly functioning human beings think flying is the most insane and illogical act a person can do. They are right. Airplanes are naturally *heavy*. They don't *look* like they could fly *anywhere*, with the possible exception of Antarctica since gravity would probably help them get down there. No, airplanes look like they'd be a lot safer just staying on the ground, and willfully strapping your body inside one, trusting it to levitate you thousands of feet above the earth, hurl you hundreds of miles through space then gently set you down again at just the right spot, is clearly a crapshoot only an adrenaline addict or Cleopatra (the Queen of Denial) could love.

So most people do not suffer from authentic Fear of Flying but acute Fear of Dying. And that never was *my* problem. Because I've been around long enough to know that nobody goes until they're supposed to go. Call it Pollyanna Precognition, but I also know that if I, or anyone else, for that matter, sign up for a flight that *is* destined for a dive and *I'm* not, I'll either survive like Michener and have a great story to tell or I'll be forewarned in some enigmatic way, as Beryl Markham was warned by her mentor, Tom Black, not to fly to Voi, a little outpost southeast of Nairobi, with Denys Finch–Hatton, whom Robert Redford played in *Out of Africa*. Markham immortalized the event in her famous autobiography, *West with the Night*:

> "Make it tomorrow, Beryl," Black had requested.
>
> "Weather?" Markham had asked.
>
> "No. The weather's all right. Just make it tomorrow— will you?"
>
> "I suppose I will, if you ask me to, but I don't see why."
>
> "Neither do I," said Tom, "but there it is."

Finch–Hatton's plane never made it back from Voi and neither did he. Markham, of course, went on, in 1936, to become the first person to fly solo across the Atlantic east to west.

No, my problem wasn't the usual white-knuckle, "We're All

Gonna Die!" business, it was more a traveler's claustrophobia—I simply could not bear to be locked in a confined space, especially if I couldn't open the windows . . . all of which made flying unspeakably uncomfortable (elevators, of course, were out of the question). As soon as the flight attendant shut the door, I panicked. The plane suddenly felt like the Serengeti, any semblance of air having instantly vanished, and my mind headed straight for "darkest" Africa. It took everything I had not to bolt from my seat, fall to my knees in front of the nearest flight attendant and *beg*, "PLEEEEASE LET ME OUTTA HERE!"

I was not, it should be explained, born with this condition. It came upon me quite suddenly in the summer of 1977 when I was a foot under water and dead. Well, I thought I was. Some friends and I had gone inner-tubing down the Willamette River in Eugene, Oregon. We were coming up to a humanmade waterfall and everyone managed to maneuver over to a little side island except *moi*, who went directly over the edge. My inner tube bounced downstream and I remained pinned under the falls, my feet caught in the churning undercurrent. No amount of dog paddling altered my position. I was stuck. And pretty soon I was out of air.

At the precise moment that I heard my own thoughts saying, "That's all, folks!" I was saved. Two strong arms fished me out by the hair then hauled me ashore. They belonged to a friend of my boyfriend-at-the-time, an architecture student who later that day taught me the word "synergy" and its meaning.

The lesson was as powerful as the trauma: Don't go in the water unless you know the river; and more profoundly, nothing can take you before your time, not even yourself. Even if *you* decide your time's up, if it really isn't, then something or someone will save you. And if your time *is* up, *nothing* can save you. *That* is divine synergy in action—life and death are, indeed, much, much grander than the sum of their visible parts.

It is ironic that this drowning experience inspired both a supreme *lack* of Fear of Dying and a deeply ingrained Fear of Flying. This contradiction was not lost on me, though it was a long time before I could raise that curtain. Trauma does that to you. It burns fear in on a lizard-brain level. Even if a near-death experience erases your Fear of Dying, it can leave you terrified of smaller things. Like Michener says, it's bad news when fear keeps you from doing what you want to do. And since, more than anything, I wanted to explore the world, Fear of Flying was definitely in my way.

Fortunately, my mother is a psychologist and she quickly explained that the horrible bouts of panic I had during the first months after my river ordeal—even a car ride would trigger them—were, in fact, bona fide Anxiety Attacks, a term I'd never heard before. She said people have them all the time for all sorts of reasons. This was comforting, in the way it is always comforting to find out you're not the only one with some weird problem, but I didn't want to have Anxiety Attacks. They were almost as bad as drowning. In fact, they were a lot *like* drowning. So my mother flew me to Los Angeles to see a psychologist friend of hers who specializes in hypnosis.

That was a Plane Trip from Hell if ever there were one. By the time I got to L.A. I looked like a chihuahua. But my hypnotist was a nice boy-next-door type with a soft spot for trauma victims. I was under in minutes and I still don't remember a thing except the post-hypnotic suggestion that whenever I felt anxious I was to place my right hand on my left shoulder, a sort of half self-hug which I find myself doing in iffy situations to this day.

Well, that helped. But it was a Band-Aid. Lock-in claustrophobia still ruled my travel plans—I still couldn't handle flying. It was time to have a little talk with myself.

"Okay," I began, "just what *are* you afraid of?"

"Being trapped," I replied firmly.

"And why are you afraid of being trapped?"

"Uh . . . because . . . I'm afraid . . . of not being able to breathe."

"Why are you afraid of not being able to breathe?" I countered swiftly, sensing a logic lapse.

"Because . . . because," I faltered. "Because I'm afraid of dying."

"But I thought you accepted dying—you said you believe your time is either up or it's not." I knew I had stumped myself with that one.

"Well . . . " I stalled. "Well, I guess I'm really afraid of . . . of being uncomfortable!" I finally blurted out.

"As in, being trapped is uncomfortable, and not being able to breathe is uncomfortable?"

"Yes," I replied. Who could quarrel with that?

"Okay," I said slowly. "If your biggest fear is being uncomfortable, WHY ARE YOU GIVING YOURSELF ANXIETY ATTACKS???"

I was right. Nothing was more uncomfortable than Anxiety Attacks. My logic made about as much sense as a screen door on a submarine. And that little epiphany was the beginning of the end.

Overnight, the Anxiety Attacks became anxiety attacks. Then they stopped. Just like that. And I never had another one, unless you count moments of sheer terror when an elevator door decides to take its own sweet time to open. But at least I was able to *take* elevators. Like airplanes, they had become a sort of occupational emotional hazard—I didn't like how they made me feel, but I took them when I had to.

By then I had discovered at my local health food store a helpful flying crutch called Rescue Remedy, a blend of English flower essences which together have a remarkably calming effect on frazzled states of mind from mild stress to all-out hysteria. Once, during that period, I actually did feel the tingling beginnings of panic on a plane, so I dripped four drops of Rescue Remedy into a little bottle of water I had in my purse and sipped it. Within *seconds* the terrible fear lifted off me like a black cloud.

I went along like that for years, flying when I had to, relying on Rescue Remedy to see me through, a practice that raises the hackles of airport security officers since X-rays destroy the delicate properties of Rescue Remedy so it has to be hand checked, and they always want to know what it is (just say "medicine").

But Rescue Remedy does not a sure cure make. The name itself tends to affirm victimhood, and if you want to get over something, at some point you have to stop thinking of yourself as its victim. Personally, I had hoped for a stronger showing upstairs. It finally arrived one good summer day when I was scheduled to fly to British Columbia on a salmon fishing assignment and for the first time I had to take a seaplane.

A friend was visiting that week, one of those rare friends you make so early in your own development that the friendship either fizzles and splits immediately, or it develops with you over time. Lauri Doyle and I had been like sisters for twenty years.

We drove, that pretty morning, to Kenmore Air Harbor at the north end of Lake Washington. The lobby was festive, filled and rushed with scores of elated travelers heading out to boreal bays and islands or returning home loaded with salmon and good stories. We all waited for our flights outside in the sun, seated like family around white picnic tables flanked with potted geraniums. Rows of yellow and brown Kenmore seaplanes bobbed at dockside— a friendlier invitation to adventure simply wasn't possible.

Nonetheless, I was pensive. These planes were *small*, only very distant cousins to the winged living rooms to which I had grown somewhat accustomed. Sure enough, when our time came to climb aboard, panic climbed aboard with me. And when the pilot shut the door, I would have gladly dived into the lake to escape.

Lauri knew what I was thinking and grabbed my knee. "You can do this," she said, then she took my arm and held on like an anchor for the next fifteen minutes. And that's when I saw it for the first time: the *real* Northwest. That soft and glorious geography, the dapple of earth on water alive with the Technicolor blues and greens that so exalt this aqueous conifer world we call our own. There it was, spread out like an altar cloth, a few hundred yards beneath my feet.

It no longer mattered that I was an anchovy packed in a tin can with wings. There was nowhere else on earth or off that I would rather be! It was a bit of quintessential Winnie-the-Pooh logic: If you want to find home in a snowstorm, don't look for it; if you don't want to feel trapped, embrace where you are.

That was the moment, there in that little single-prop De Havilland Beaver, winging up the west coast of Whidbey Island, when the veil finally lifted, revealing the link between the release of fear and the celebration of your own life's life, moment by holy moment. From then on, the roar of a plane, especially a seaplane, has triggered nothing in me but excitement, the raw, sweet joy of imminent adventure. And I understand why, when I asked him why the rest of the world should know Alaska, James Michener described seeing it by plane. "You fly from Prudhoe Bay to Barrow along the Arctic seacoast and see maybe 5,000 lakes down below! Or you fly over Southeast Alaska—I think there are 10,000 islands there. There's really nothing like it." And why Beryl Markham wrote, after her own maiden flight: "I saw the alchemy of perspective reduce my world to grains in a cup."

When the wind kicked up over the Georgia Strait that remarkable day, and our little plane convulsed and bucked, Fear of Dying spread like cholera amongst the passengers, with the exception of Lauri, who is the original daredevil, and myself, who had by then become the wind. And, of course, the spirit of Beryl Markham. She had died in Nairobi the week before, a half-century after she crash-landed in the Nova Scotia mud and emerged with nothing more than a bump on her triumphant head.

The Ritual of Winter Steelhead

"Wild steelhead are like the temperate rain forest," Guido was saying. "They evolved together. And they've become endangered together."

Guido Rahr is a connoisseur of both forest and fish. And rivers, for that matter. A native Oregonian, he lives in Portland, where his main work is developing strategies to help protect wild salmon and steelhead. Otherwise, he fishes Northwest rivers every chance he gets—something he's done all his life. I am convinced that if you are, say, the Lucille

Ball of fly-casting, your only prayer is to sign up with a guy like Guido and hope that somewhere downstream, a fraction of his finesse, control and expertise suddenly leaps lightning-like from his rod to yours in one of the great Benjamin Franklin Electricity Demonstrations of the twentieth century.

It was Sunday. I headed south out of Seattle in the dark and watched the sunrise turn the Nisqually farmlands into an Andrew Wyeth painting. Plumes of morning fog rose off the land like God's breath. The celestial light sent pink blessings down the backs of the rivers I passed—the Skookumchuck and the Toutle, even the Kalama, wriggling like a trapped snake beneath the poison tower of its now-defunct nuclear plant. If ever there were a day for miracles, for a total klutz to finally master the delicate art of fly-casting, this was it.

I picked up Guido, then we doubled back into Washington looking for the wagging tail of a certain tributary of the Lewis River which I am not at liberty to divulge under penalty of never getting another fishing lesson as long as I live. Guido's pal, Tom Scott, followed, pulling a McKenzie River drift boat he'd built himself.

"No guidebooks will tell you about the secret streams of Oregon and Washington," Guido instructed. "You have to teach yourself. Get out there and ask around. And when you discover one, guard it. It's a precious thing."

We turned into the parking lot of The Tackle Box, a source

of "bait, tackle and hunting supplies" and daily reports on steelhead hot spots. The fish were in the river all right. The shop's walls were covered with recent Polaroids of grinning fishermen holding up steelhead as long as your leg.

"Jeez! Half of these are wild fish," Guido said. "See, you can tell because their adipose fins aren't clipped. . . . They should have released them."

It is one of the great natural ironies that the greatest fishermen become the greatest protectors of fish. When you adore the ancient art of fly-fishing, its demands and its beauty, the gambler's hope of it—when you are as hooked as any fish ever was—then you become, if your brain even remotely approaches the size of a salmon egg, a rabid conservationist. You cannot imagine life without salmon or trout. Or steelhead, which are, in fact, ocean-going rainbow trout. You can't bear the thought of living through the season without regular expeditions into the honest countryside around your home, in patient pursuit of the grand and mysterious water beings that live there.

It was England's Izaak Walton who insisted that fly-fishing was the only true Western meditation. It is, as well, the Northwest's truest obsession, and this fact alone might, in the end, save our native fish from extinction, if enough regional fishermen, both sporting and commercial, can finally connect the dots between love and supply, and agree to put some restraint where their egos and wallets have always been.

"I just love this river," Guido said. "Its steelhead are spectacular, sometimes more than twenty pounds. They're also a threatened species—every year, less and less come back."

It was winter and the river was running like a banshee, a gift of the great rains. I considered the swimming properties of my waders, which weren't great. Mainly because they weren't my waders. They belonged to a friend, a man who is a lot taller than I am. Being a salmon fisherwoman by training, I had taken a casting lesson from him two days earlier so Guido wouldn't send me downstream in a leaky canoe, and my pal had, with characteristic generosity, set me up with a fine Winston fly rod, as well as a Sage, and reels, waders, boots, an English fly case and a set of glorious flies he'd tied himself. "That ought to impress this Guido guy," he said.

Guido was impressed. Then he produced the flies we would fish, which he'd tied himself—that's how fly-fishermen are. They were pretty little things—with bodies of braided iridescent green "Flashaboo," coral yarn throats, three wraps of soft grizzly hackle—from a chicken, not a bear—and gray squirrel tails. They were supposed to look like little shrimp. Guido thought steelhead would love them. I knew *I'd* eat them if I were a fish . . . or at least make earrings out of them. I named them the Scampi.

Before Tom could get his boat in the water, Guido had stomped off downstream. He crossed the river, which, mercifully, was shallower than it looked, and began casting. I stomped off after him and instantly fell in. My boots were a men's size nine. My feet swam around in them while *they* swam around on the slippery rocks—sort of a swim-swim situation.

Finally, I found my footing and got my Scampi airborne. It hung up in the cattails behind me, and I stomped back to free it and fell in. I stomped back to my fishing spot and got my Scampi in the water this time. It hung up on the first rock it got close to. I stomped upriver to tug it loose and fell in. At this point Guido yelled. He had a fish on. It was his third cast.

It is invaluable to study a master fly-fisherman play a fish. He will remain hunched over and so will his rod tip, the tension between it and the fish perfect always. When the fish runs, the fisherman drops his rod tip and lets it run. The fish rolls and the fisherman steps sideways in the same direction, then when the fish rests, the fisherman pulls his rod tip to the side to keep the fish off-balance, to keep him moving. When, finally, the fish tires, the fisherman reels it in, a little at a time. There is no force, only response. No impatience, only sensitivity. The entire event exists only as a mirrored dance that takes precisely as long as it takes. It's a good thing fishermen don't make love the way they fish or women would never let them out of bed long enough to go fishing.

Steelhead are the largest rainbow trout on earth. They evolved in the temperate rain forest where rivers are so thoroughly flushed by the great rains that they learned to swim out into the ocean for food. They travel incredible distances—farther than most salmon—and have been netted as far away as Siberia. Of the 195 native, naturally spawning salmon, steelhead and sea-run cutthroat trout stocks in the Northwest and northern California, 90 face a high risk of extinction.

Guido's fish was a beauty. A nine-pound hatchery steelhead. I had never seen one before, and in this pale season its coloring was stunning. The scales flashed subtle prisms—lemon and lilac, teal and peach. A bright crimson rose bloomed in its cheek and a hot magenta stem flashed down its flank. Guido held it just long enough for photographs, then set it free. It vanished like pink lightning.

Watching someone catch a major fish in the first five minutes of a fishing trip would be like watching the Seahawks score five touchdowns in the first quarter—whatever happens next doesn't matter much. Under Tom's excellent oarsmanship, we drifted the length of the Lewis, tying up, wading and fishing as we went. Tom is a fine fly-fisherman too, but neither he nor Guido caught another steelhead. I, however, caught many things—a tree branch, a rock, a wiggling little minitrout about three inches long. I slopped along, trying like thunder to cast my line, but it just landed in a loopy mess.

Finally, I stopped. And looked downstream at Tom and Guido. Their motions were smooth. They weren't whipping the sky. What they were doing looked more like painting, like drawing a line in the air above your head. A line that undulated, something akin to a shifting of hips. Dancer that I am, *that* I knew I could do.

I tried again. Holding my rod without the earlier fierceness, I took it back only to one o'clock and waited a beat, as Guido had instructed a dozen times, then I took it forward, then—just for practice—I took it back again. My line sailed. It painted. And when I took it forward again and let it go, the Scampi landed gracefully a good twenty feet off the tip, the line floating straight and true on the water behind it.

I tried it again. Again it worked. And again. And again. I felt like a cowgirl about to lasso a pony. Leonard Bernstein calling forth the flutes. Mickey Mouse in Merlin's robes, directing the magic brooms. I felt like Desi instead of Lucy, doing a mean tango in the winter vapors above the cool, green dance floor of the river.

God Dogs

The Chena River twisted below us like a snake in a hawk's talon. It was an odd shade, as if God had melted down sage and jade and several tree frogs then poured the new color hot across the Alaskan permafrost. The land around it thinned and opened up into puddles of coffee-colored lake ringed with chartreuse bushes. The moss beside them had gone all crimson while some other undecipherable vegetation remained a determined mauve despite the color's post-eighties pariah status. Dark triangles of Black and Sitka spruce anchored yellow rectangles of picture-perfect birch trees which, from the air, looked like buttes of grated lemon. It was such a painted landscape I had trouble believing that in a month it would all be the color of blanched almonds. Winter was coming. And this high-toned autumn route from Fairbanks west over the Minto Flats and on to Eureka Creek would soon be a musher's paradise, the personal highway of Susan Butcher, Iditarod champion extraordinaire, whom I was about to meet.

"You know mushers," Jack the pilot was saying. "I like 'em, but you wouldn't want to live next door to one. They've got a lot of dogs that yowl a lot. But they do try to live out where they won't bother anybody."

And where they can go dogsledding right out their back doors eight months of the year. Which is why Susan Butcher lives in the middle of Alaska's snowbound heart, the perfect arterial for dogs that love to run and women who love to run them.

The Flats became forest and stayed that way for the better part of one air hour. Then a road cut a pale incision across the evergreens and two compounds appeared beneath us about a quarter mile apart.

"I don't know which one's hers," Jack said. "We'll fly over both houses and let 'em know we're here."

We did, then Jack took the little Cessna down on an airstrip that should have been a parking space. His jaw muscles ticked the whole time.

"Whew," he said once we finally landed. "A little work there."

"Too short?"

"Windy."

Someone had warned him about the strip's bizarre crosswinds. When we got out of the plane they almost took our hair off. All around us tall bushes rattled out their cold, irregular pulse. But the chill died in the sun's wake, a giddy roast of morning heat. It was a glorious day.

Eventually David Munson came to fetch us in an old pickup. Six years ago to the day he had married Susan Butcher, then moved with her to the Alaskan bush where there is, he says, "a distinct lack of distractions from trivialities like, 'Which Hallmark card should I buy?'" He quit his law practice to run the business side of his wife's magnificent dog-racing obsession. Which is, first, an obsession with dogs. More than 120 of them. All Alaskan huskies. All tethered to wooden posts and yowling out an inspired doggie devotional to their best pal in the world who was, at the moment, striding toward her 1910 blacksmith's log cabin where I sat staring at the eight-inch tooth still embedded in the mastodon jaw that hung above the bedroom door.

This is not, I was thinking, the home of a Sybarite, or even a nest-featherer. And certainly not an upwardly aimed, shopping-junkie lawyer's wife. There was no running water, no electricity, no phone. A propane lamp hung from the ceiling, a wood stove stood in for central heating and the only art in the place was a yellow Iditarod Trail decal on the oven and a beautiful 1978 Machetanz watercolor of a musher and his dogs called *Coming into the Home Stretch*.

The sofa and armchair were that throw-a-bedspread-over-it brand everyone has in college, and the chipped linoleum floor was not allergic to snow and mud. Or dogs. Which was the point. This cabin was dog-proof. Neat, clean, cozy, sufficient . . . and dog-proof. The line between Susan Butcher's outdoor and indoor lives was dog-hair thin. To her, God was dog spelled backwards and not the other way around.

In honor of my visit, though I was surely a suspected City Slicker Nerdette, Susan had baked a sourdough coffee cake. I wanted to blurt out that I live in a log cabin too, on an almost rural island, with four cats, seven rabbits and a bunch of wild pheasant, deer and owls, even a neighboring bald eagle. I wanted to tell her that I fish and kayak and attend Audubon meetings and follow wild animals around every chance I get. But it was only half-true. I'm only half Wild Woman—the other half is as devoted to art and culture as Susan is to her dogs. I was wearing red lipstick, for chrissake. Compared to Susan, I am, I had to admit, a Wilderness Wimp, a real Outdoor Oreo—firm on the outside, smooshy on the inside. I don't even drink coffee.

"Coffee? . . . or tea?" Susan asked. I confessed to tea and relief flooded her face. "Great!" she said. "I don't know how to make coffee."

Her long twin braids swung like reins behind her as she filled the kettle from a tub of hauled-in water. She moved fast, like a hyper-oxygenated athlete, and it was easy to believe that she could vaporize any obstacle in her path just by zapping it with the wild wolf light that glitters always in her sky-colored eyes.

"This was a wolf's territory when we moved here," she said, reading my thoughts again. "Over four years I lost six puppies. It was awful, terrible . . . but we *had* invaded the wolf's home. He finally either left or died."

It was clear that Susan Butcher knows her place in the natural world like few humans do. And that nature and her dogs are her truest mentors.

"I always take moral decisions back to what animals would do in the wild—what is right and what is natural," she said. "The more you live around animals, the more you communicate on that psychic level—they teach you so much about instincts you've lost. With one of my dogs, Tekla, I just have to *think* 'gee,' which is right, or 'haw,' which is left, and she'll turn that way."

The Telepathic WATS Line runs both ways. Once, while on a ten-day climb on Mt. McKinley, Susan had three separate dreams about a fire breaking out in her kennel back home. "When David picked me up after the climb," she said, "he told me a forest fire had been raging five miles from the cabin the whole time I was gone."

Her dreams were vivid, her terror was real. "It was like 120 of your best friends were about to burn to death. Most people don't *have* 120 best friends. But I know *everything* about each of my dogs. They're my family, friends and workmates, and we all put in twelve- to sixteen-hour work days."

Running a thousand miles from Anchorage to Nome in the middle of an Alaskan winter takes some serious talent. And conditioning. Like any athlete, the core daily activity of Susan's dogs is training. They're fed and watered five times a day and they're brushed. "We race every day, too," she said. "It's a shame you didn't get here earlier because I was planning to take you mushing this morning, but it's too hot now. We use dirt trails until it snows," she added, noting what must have looked like an extremely confused expression.

It was really a hybrid of disbelief and devastation. Susan Butcher was planning to take *me* mushing!? And I missed it!? And to think I had waited at the Tamarak Air office for an hour that morning while Jack flew some demanding client around overtime. I wanted to scream, but I just said: "I love dogsledding."

I had, in fact, done a little mushing in Alberta, Canada—a sort of dogsledding day trip. My long-time best pal, Rande Lisle, came with me. When we climbed into the sled and I admitted feeling guilty about letting dogs haul me across the snow all day, it was Rande who insisted that the dogs *loved* to mush. "Listen," she said. "They're singing!"

They were, in fact, making a joyful noise, a yipping, yodeling canine chorus that didn't let up until Doug Hannah, their kindly owner, cried, "Hee-yaw!" and we were off. Dashing through the snow, in a nine-dog open sleigh, over the fields we'd go, laughing all the way . . . because Rande kept saying things like, "Does the sled ever go faster than the dogs?" and "I can't believe they can go to the bathroom at a dead run!" and "Do dogs attract bears?"

Alpine firs whirred by, the mountain air filled our faces with the refrigerated perfume of winter, and the northern Rockies were our companions all the way to the lodge, where a good hot lunch awaited us. The dog team, Rande pointed out, had smiled the whole way.

I knew then why Susan Butcher was so in love with mushing. And with her dogs. Sled dogs are working dogs, obliging and true. Exuberant, Susan would say, but well-behaved. They want to see the world as much as you do. They live to go. They don't hold back. They want to know where each moment can take them and they never worry about hungry bears or full-winter white-out blizzards. Sled dogs are a living act of faith, and their enthusiasm is highly infectious. They remind you, without judgement, how much your own fears make you shy away from the Great Adventure that is your life.

"I don't have any actual fears, *but* I have a lot of educated respect for danger," Susan will tell you. "Open water, small planes, and I'm not fond of running into angry moose. . . . But I'm ready to die." She means it.

"I thought I was dead once. A friend and I crashed in a small plane, but we walked away and so did the pilot. We were lost for three days. It was *cold*, and we had no water—you had to dig to find something moist to suck on. There was no food, just a lot of berries, and a *lot* of bears—we had no firearms," she said, grinning. "The pilot thought it was the worst thing that had ever happened to him. But my friend and I had been working so hard it was like a vacation. And, I had my pet fox with me. . . . "

A dogsled of sorrow suddenly raced across her eyes. The animal, clearly, was no longer with her, and I didn't want to ask. Then, with her usual telepathic panache, Susan Butcher said almost impatiently, "Death is part of country life. You don't have 120 dogs and not see death. And so many friends die from drowning out here, or in plane crashes. I've held people in my arms for six hours while they died, and it's not scary. It's sad. And you grieve. But it's *not* scary. The fear comes from a lack of understanding."

We walked outside and played with some puppies in a nearby pen. They watched Susan's every move with their opaque glacier eyes and licked her face when she bent down to scratch them. In the early fall light it looked like an Alaskan home movie, and for some reason I asked Susan about her fan letters.

"Oh, the letters!" she sang. "They make me cry and cry and

cry. People write and say that what *I'm* doing gives *them* the strength to do what *they* want to do. One woman wrote that just getting to the grocery store was her Iditarod. She has cancer, and she says if she thinks of me, she can do it."

Granite, Susan's famous now-retired lead dog, strolled over and put his head on her knee and I could only guess at the depth of their connection—the victories they won, the chances they took, the miles they raced, the life they led. Suddenly, my own small risks didn't seem so small, not for a brotherless city girl with Barbie dolls as role models. I *did* leave the city to live in the country. I *do* raise animals and I *do* go fishing in water that would gladly eat you for breakfast. I've made it my business to go Out There whenever I can, where the elk bugle and the bison run and the skies are not cloudy all day. And I'm not afraid to fly 150 miles in a very small plane over very serious bear country to spend three hours with a woman whose very existence made me feel proud that I had.

That, I think, is Susan Butcher's great gift: to inspire wholly by example because, like her dogs, she is entirely what she appears to be. And she can bake one mean sourdough coffee cake, too. With the kind of grace that only comes from accepting and rejoicing in who you really are, lipstick and all, I asked Susan if I could come back and go mushing with her once it snowed. And she grinned that wonderful, exuberant, this-is-it grin, and said, "Sure."

The Tyee Club

We'd been fishing about five minutes when a cannibal wind came screaming out of the north and started slapping our rowboat around. Then Discovery Passage blew up in our faces, splattering the air with violent black stew. It happened in seconds. It always does at dawn up there on the 50th parallel in that narrow raceway between Vancouver and Quadra Islands off the fractured coast of British Columbia, a place joined at the latitudinal hip with England's Land's End, Newfoundland and Siberia. January, August—it doesn't matter. The local Kwagiulth Indians knew that at any moment the Cannibal at the North End of the World could hiss his icy breath south and turn their sacred fishing grounds into a real man-eater.

Rich sucked the rain out of his moustache. "Thirteen pulls," he said, but the wind ate his words. I had fished this demented water a hundred times, so I took a guess and sunk a dozen arm lengths of line into that evil soup, praying that Rich's double-clinch knot and his antique Lucky Louie lure would have a lasting relationship. I also prayed that I would, after all these years, finally fish myself into The Tyee Club of British Columbia.

The Tyee Club was founded in 1924 by exceptionally sporting anglers who realized that exceptional fish need exceptional protection from run-of-the-mill yahoos who would take every last one by any means possible if you let them. So the Tyee Club laid down a few ground rules to give the colossal salmon I have personally pursued for the better part of a decade "a sporting chance." Under Tyee Club regulations you can, for instance, only fish out of a rowboat—no motors allowed. You may use only a hand-operated reel, your line must have a breaking strength of twenty pounds or less, and you are allowed only a single-hook, artificial trolling lure—bait is strictly forbidden. And the only way to get into the Tyee Club is to boat a thirty-pound or better "tyee" salmon using regulation tackle and tactics. After seven years and God knows how many tides, I had only managed to land an infuriatingly close twenty-seven pounder. Thus had I become a woman possessed, and no steenking Cannibal breath was going to keep me off the holy water that Native American and non-Native American alike call the Tyee Pool.

Tyee is a word borrowed from the old Chinook jargon used between Native Americans and early white traders all along the Northwest coast. It means "chief," and that's what the original tribes named the biggest Pacific salmon, the species we now call "chinook." It was no overstatement. For at least 8,500 years—that's 4,000 years before the pyramids were built—Pacific Northwest Indians counted on salmon like we count on McDonald's. It was salmon that supported a prehistoric population of 50,000 from Puget Sound to Southeast Alaska, *without* an agricultural base. So when a Kwagiulth fisherman handlined a sixty-pound tyee into his dugout canoe, you can bet he was humming his version of "Hail to the Chief."

Some of British Columbia's biggest tyees come out of the Campbell River, which empties into Discovery Passage just beneath the nipple of Vancouver Island's long, lean east coast, some 170 road miles north of Victoria. If you ever happen to snorkel down the Campbell you'll see why it produces such lunkers. Thanks to the filtering action of upstream waterfalls, the riverbed is filled with fist-sized rocks. Cobble rock, they call it. And since spawning female salmon dig their nests—or redds—some seventeen inches into the gravel, the old Campbell self-selected eons ago for big mothers with Terminator-tails. The result was a run of tyee that routinely weighed-in at forty, fifty, even seventy pounds—tens of pounds larger than the salmon of neighboring rivers.

Fossils prove that salmonoids have run in the Northwest for five million years, the wily survivors of many Ice Ages. Ever since the last one about 11,000 years ago, Campbell River salmon have spent their summer vacations cruising the Tyee Pool while they transmogrified from saltwater predators into freshwater spawning machines . . . which is why Rich Chapple, tyee fishing guide extraordinaire, and I were sitting in a boat the size of a hot tub half an hour before sunrise, fishing blind in weather that could rip the fur off King Kong . . . all for the love of these impertinent fish that have about as much interest in eating as Dick Gregory.

"Whoa!" Rich hollered as one porpoised inches from our boat. Its splash spritzed me in the face. "That's good luck," Rich said, and he ought to know. In his early guiding career, he used to eat the heart of every tyee his clients caught . . . raw.

Tyee salmon are, in fact, almost impossible to catch. That's because they are interested in sex. By the time they enter the dilute saltwater of the Tyee Pool, their stomachs have shrunk to the size of a lug nut as their bodies fill with the procreational cargo needed for the lusty last act of their lives. It is an aggressive, if subgustatory, time in a salmon's life. Males fight males for mates, females prepare to defend their once and future redds. Thus, an angler's only chance is to bonk an already semi-pissed-off tyee on the head with a ridiculous imitation of a squid or a herring and hope the little Pliocene devil bites it out of sheer irritability.

In Discovery Passage, the morning tide is usually an ebb like the one Rich was fighting. Given the geography of the place, ebb tides flow north, and set up a curious back-eddy in the pool as they pass. They also move faster than you can row, so we were doing what's called an "ebb drift," starting at the south end of the Tyee Pool, rowing hard against the current, but still drifting north toward the river's mouth along the edge of what's called the Bar, which is where the fish are. The tyee are holding near the bottom, working against the current, too—finning, really, to stay in one place like they do in a river, sort of a dress rehearsal for their upcoming performance in the Campbell. The idea is that as you drift the ebb, your lure does an annoying little jig down below in front of every fish face it meets, and eventually one of them is going to go for it and you're gonna get lucky.

It takes a lot of skill to row an ebb, especially in cannibal weather. That's why it's so important to have a guide who knows what he or she's doing, one who has a blueprint of the bottom of the Tyee Pool etched on his or her brain and is well-versed in the locations of the Corner, the Bar and other famous Tyee Pool salmon hangouts. You also want a guide with a good collection of classic tyee tackle who knows which plug or spoon to row on which tide and how to row it.

Tyee tackle is one of the sport's great mysteries. A tyee angler cannot, for instance, gather together fifty kinds of hackle and herl, then whip up a Jock Scott fly guaranteed to attract the bejesus out of an Atlantic salmon and expect it to have the same effect on a British Columbia tyee. It won't. Nothing will. Attraction has nothing to do with it. Aggravation does, which is why the Quasimodo spaz-attacks of plugs and spoons work so well.

Unlike fly patterns, which can be reproduced ad infinitum, tyee lures are one-of-a-kind pieces of proven art that fish best in specific kinds of water, the beginning of the ebb, for instance, or the end of the flood. The preferred tyee plug is called a Lucky Louie, a piece of wood or plastic, painted white and shaped like a Conehead larva. The preferred Lucky Louie is called a plastic Shovel-nose, a 1950s design whose dished-out face really rocks in a strong current.

The best tyee tackle is as old as your average baby boomer and has been fished for decades. Many have names: the White Witch, for instance (a silver-plated spoon), Uncle Dick (a Shovel-nose), Bland (a very pale Shovel-nose), Blue Rhonda (a Lucky Louie supposedly named after a sexual fantasy) or the Juggler (another Shovel-nose and a gift from Paul Magid, a Flying Karamazov Brother with a serious fishing habit). Since two clients can fish out of a rowboat at the same time, a guide also needs a couple of lures that fish well together, as in the case of one famous pair of spoons that sets up such a goofy cross-rhythm their owner knighted them the Marx Brothers.

Tyee guides consider all this hallowed hardware their most prized possession. They guard their plugs and spoons like gold, trade them like stock and give them to each other for wedding presents. They are heroically generous in loaning them to their clients, but God help the witless angler who loses one—the guilt alone will mess up your concentration for days.

At the moment, we were fishing Rich's hottest plug, a plastic Shovel-nose named Jesus Murphy after what Rich said when veteran tyee guide Scott Laird gave it to him for his birthday. My job was to focus Buddha-like attention on my rod tip while it telegraphed the subaquatic activity of my lure which, under normal conditions, rides the currents of the Tyee Pool like a waltzing heartbeat. But this extra-weird wave action was making Jesus Murphy hip-hop all over the place. If a tyee hit it, I'd be the last to know, especially since the morning was still roughly the color of the interior of a whale and I couldn't see a damn thing.

The storm was so bad that Rich, who is six foot six and has guided in the pool for twenty years, was having trouble just keeping *Lucky*, his rowboat, from doing another 180. He had to row directly into the wind in order to maintain any position at all, which gets especially complicated when you consider that rowboats go backwards to begin with. The only thing that made any sense that morning was Taj Mahal's grits-and-catfish voice blowing blue smoke out of my pink boom box which we had crammed into a Hefty Bag for the occasion.

The first Anglo account of tyee fishing, "A Seventy Pound Salmon with Rod and Line," was written by Sir Richard Musgrave of the British Royal Navy and published in the October 1896 issue of *The Field*, London's prestigious sporting magazine. In it Musgrave meticulously describes his five-day Campbell River tyee adventure. Fishing with a Native-American guide out of a dugout canoe, Musgrave and a friend took nineteen tyee weighing a total of 894 pounds. On the day he boated his seventy-pounder, he and his buddy also took a fifty- and a forty-seven-pound salmon . . . all before lunch.

In his handsome book, *TYEE: The Story of the Tyee Club of British Columbia*, Campbell River writer Van Gorman Egan reports that Musgrave fought his seventy-pound fish "for an hour and three-quarters in a swift current" which he claims carried him nearly three miles down the coast. "My left hand was trembling so much that I could hardly put a cigarette in my mouth," Musgrave wrote. "An old golf glove, too, was quite cut through by the line, and I had great difficulty saving my fingers."

Egan claims Musgrave's story "heralded an angler's migration to Campbell River which has not abated to this day." Indeed, they came from Egypt, Australia, New York, and many from the British Isles, all arriving by steamer with a full camp and high hopes of landing a Campbell River chief. In 1904, a hotel called the Willows was built on the shore of the Tyee Pool to accommodate these hoards of Anglo anglers willing to freeze their knickers off for the chance to land a salmon as tall as their wife.

Inevitably, somebody got greedy. In 1908, over a period of two weeks, one Frank Griswold took forty-seven tyee averaging forty-two pounds apiece with a tarpon rod, fifty-pound test line and a Vom Hofe reel that a witness claimed carried "a drag that would stop a buffalo."

Egan assures us that it was Griswold's own unrestrained accounts of his tyee triumphs that attracted Zane Grey to the Campbell River in 1919. A veteran of California's famous Tuna Club of Catalina Island, Grey set out to prove that these jumbo salmon could be taken with light tackle, a method that had recently been pioneered for tuna fishing. Thus, he produced a rod with an astonishing six-ounce tip and a reel with wimpy nine-thread line, not the then standard twenty-one.

"How long will this hold a tyee?" Grey asked a Native-American man named Jim.

"About two minutes," Jim replied. Grey hired him on the spot as his guide.

Zane Grey's methods turned out to be so successful that light tackle became one of the Tyee Club's hallmarks. But it wasn't he who helped found the club, it was his favorite fishing buddy, a man who appears in many Zane Grey fishing stories simply as "Lone Angler."

Meeting at the Willows Hotel in 1924, three of the world's first fish conservationists decided to form the Tyee Club—A. N. Wolverton of Vancouver, British Columbia, the hotel's manager, Melville Haigh, and Lone Angler himself, one Dr. J. A. Wiborn. They decreed right there on the banks of the Tyee Pool that the Club's rules would "do everything possible to conserve for all time the fine run of this outstanding species of salmon."

At the moment, the Cannibal was doing a real decent job of it all by his unholy self. Stiletto torrents assaulted our rain gear from all directions while Rich cranked on the oars like the athlete he is.

"Oh, I wish I were an Oscar Meyer wiener!" he sang in his fine sailor's baritone. "Because then I'd be at a picnic instead of rowing this frigging bo-o-oat."

He wasn't the only one. All around us, tyee guides wrestled with the storm while their boats' red and green running lights jumped in the blackness like Christmas-in-a-blender. Normally, pre-dawn tyee fishing is a balm, the water a gel, and the only sound that breaks the quiet is the lapping rhythm of the oars and the occasional watery burst and descending slap of a leaping salmon. But in this noisy chaos, the one steadying force that galvanized us all was the anticipation of the Moment, which would, we knew, soon be upon us . . . we just didn't know exactly when. You never do.

Usually, it occurs just when your mind decides to take a powder. You were thinking about breakfast. You were thinking about sex (this *is* spawning water). You were thinking about *anything* but the invisible tip of your rod. Shut up. Pay attention. Any moment could be the Moment, you idiot. Then the thin gold ribbon of sunrise giftwraps the shark-tooth skyline of Quadra Island directly east of you, and the morning goes pink. First Light. You are fishing now in the thinnest of air, under a sky like bleached opals, in water like grape jelly. Finally, you can see. The Cannibal backs off a little, the ice pick rain turns to soft needles and you note that the tip of your rod is, in fact, nodding away like Ray Charles.

There is a flotilla of twenty-five rowboats in the pool now. Everyone staring at their rod tip. Everyone quiet. Everyone cold and wet as a clam. Somewhere behind you a seaplane takes off, and in that hanging drone your mind finally implodes. Sound unites. Boundaries blur. Waterskyboatfishguide.

Trout fishing has its morning and evening bites. These are fairly regular events which have to do with the circadian rhythm of insects, the natural feeding cycles of fish and an angler's innate glee in vexing his or her spouse. But the only thing remotely predictable about tyee fishing is that almost every morning, usually just before or just after or even an hour after dawn, but not usually an hour before because there's almost never anyone out fishing that early to find out . . . all of a sudden, for no good reason, the fish decide to go for it. Bam! One hits a line five boats to the north. Bam! Bambambam! Another hits two boats due west and two more hit the boat off your stern, then a reel sings right behind you. That is how the Moment happens.

The problem is, it usually doesn't happen to you. Tyee are gifts not given lightly. Or often. And of the five or so that may hit, perhaps three will make it to the boat without breaking off—that's the built-in conservationism of tyee fishing. That's why you put in your rod hours, summer after summer after summer. Not only is there the incentive of feeling the slam-dunk, over-the-wall, out-of-the-park, long-bomb bite of a tyee salmon stripping your line to Japan, and, of course, the draw of becoming a bona fide member of the Tyee Club, but there is also the little matter of collecting Tyee Club buttons, handsome pins for your hat or lapel that are as authentic as Ralph Lauren isn't, all awarded based on the weight of your fish. You get a bronze for a thirty-pounder, silver for a forty, gold for a fifty, diamond for a sixty and the coveted ruby button for a seventy, only two of which have been given in the history of the Tyee Club.

That summer the gift of a tyee almost was mine, or, rather, Rich's, since the role of the guide is so key to catching a serious salmon that Campbell River etiquette considers any tyee taken to be the guide's, who is said to have "guided the fish."

When the pink snake of morning crawled across the eastern sky it was as if Salmon Woman herself had cast a glamour over everything, a metallic wash that made the passage and the air, the mountains, even the pulp mill to the north, gleam like living salmon skin that vanishes as soon as the fish leaves the water. I couldn't stand it any longer.

"I feel lucky," I said out loud.

"Me too," Rich replied.

Before my Lucky Louie could nod in agreement a fish hit it so hard I had no choice but to wake up and smell the coffee which I had just spilled all over my boots. Fortunately, I hit the rod as hard as the fish had, much to Rich's amazement. To this day he calls my reaction "some kind of ethereal instinct." That's the first trick to landing a tyee—setting the hook hard the split-nanosecond you feel a bite. You'd rip the lips off a trout if you set a hook like that while fly-fishing, but you have to do it with a salmon whose head is about the size of a large dog's.

The rest is the eternal tango of fisherman and fish, but in this case you have to let the fish lead. If you've got a grand slam chinook on your line, the first thing it's going to do is run for all its worth. Let it. You *have* to let it. Because a spawning salmon that size possesses a locomotive power unlike any other you're likely to encounter, especially on light tackle. And if you *don't* let it run, it will simply snap your line like so much raw spaghetti, a heartbreak even Zane Grey learned the hard way.

" . . . after three minutes Grey felt the fish would be his," Van Egan writes. "Having seen it on the surface he estimated its weight at over fifty pounds. With increasing confidence, misplaced, he would learn to his later sorrow, he worked the fish hard, stopping two runs 'at will,' and pumping it with 'long lifts of the rod.' To this the immense fish rushed to the surface, thrashing wildly and the hook tore out."

"How I regretted it!" Grey confessed afterward.

My own reel shrieked like a bagpipe playing in fast forward, and all I could do was keep my fingers away from its "knuckle buster" handles and commence the sport's hymnlike call-and-response. My fish ran fast and I let it, keeping my rod tip up and my line taut at all times because a slack line is an open invitation to a thrown hook. Then, when I felt the slightest pause in the salmon's flight, I reeled in hard, praying it wasn't one of the Tyee Pool's intellectual warriors who turn suddenly and run toward the boat, making your line go so slack so fast you can expect to reel in an empty hook.

The salmon took another long run, shattering the surface of the water this time and presenting its silveriness to the born-again sky. Rich was convinced it was at least a thirty-pounder and my heart soared like a Quadra Island eagle.

Thus I played the fish. Run, reel in, run, reel in, and finally, when it tired, reel-reel-reel, all the way home. Thirty minutes later, biceps burning way beyond the Jane Fonda comfort zone, I carefully maneuvered the fish to *Lucky's* starboard side and Rich netted it perfectly.

Then there was the Second Moment. The one no one likes to talk about. The moment your glorious opponent lies panting at your feet, longer and heavier than your leg, out of its element and out of air, and you are supposed to be very happy. While your guide reaches for his club, you watch in sorrow as that indescribable opalescent salmon-shine fades from your fish's flank, replaced in seconds by a gray haze as dull as the smoke from the upstream mill that often ruins the morning sky. "Steady," you think. "Remember, the run is not endangered and you eat fish. And this is the most honorable way to stock your larder."

Rich gave the thing a single, expert, lethal blow and I thought of the Kalahari Bushman in *The Gods Must Be Crazy*, kneeling beside his fallen antelope, hand on horn, explaining that his people needed meat and thanking it for letting them have it. Then there was the somewhat embarrassing question of whether or not this fish would get me into the Tyee Club, which Rich, seeing him up close, was beginning to doubt.

Sure enough, it was a pound and a half light. But it was a male and he was most certainly a thing of beauty. Even in death, his colors shimmered, and his geometry was astounding. The line from his nose to his dorsal fin ran ruler straight, giving him a profile more like a Roman god's than a salmon's. Back at the lodge, Eiji San, a gyotako fish print maker, pronounced him the most beautiful salmon he'd ever seen. The print still hangs proudly in my living room.

That fish didn't get me into the Tyee Club. We had a good time—you always do when you go tyee fishing—and there's nothing like a cannibal wind to make you appreciate breakfast. But even Ruby, the tyee rod Rich built just for me, has not yet managed to pull a serious salmon out of the Tyee Pool.

I still believe she will some day. And so I go. Summer after summer, year after year, sitting dutifully in *Lucky* on mornings the color of eels, holding my excellent tyee rod with hands like frozen squid while my mascara runs like squid ink, waiting for the moment my Shovel-nose Louie dances one too many times down the Tyee Pool and a monster of a Pacific salmon finally goes ballistic and the champagne water of Discovery Passage says to the beautiful black sky, "Throw your big leg up over me, mama, I might never feel this good again."

River Music

From the bank, the river looked like a snake, glistening green and sliding through the rocks. I couldn't see its fangs, but I knew they were there, waiting for me just around the next bend, sharp, white and dangerous—the Rapids. I was scared.

Hell hath no terror like that of those-who-have-almost-drowned, which I had in a river long ago, young, foolish and in the company of similarly moronic friends, one of whom somehow managed to rescue me at the exact moment I had surrendered to the death-god of the river.

The ordeal left me deeply marked by the power of white water, and I had avoided it ever since. But now, I knew, my number was up. I had, after all, lived an adventurous life. Being a nature writer by profession, I had been obliged to kayak in deadly storms, hike rattlesnake-ridden ridges, track moose through blizzards, crouch just inches from stampeding buffalo, overcome my fear of flying, fish alongside Alaska brown bear, swim with whales, snorkel with salmon . . . why, I had even camped on the steppes of Outer Mongolia with the local pit vipers, one of whom decided to make an unscheduled appearance in my neighbor's bedroll. Clearly, I was out of excuses. The old rookie-in-the-wilderness routine was a leaky canoe without a paddle. It was time to make peace with the grim river reaper.

So there I was, standing in the bleached morning light of an Idaho August with the worst forest fires in a decade breathing dragon breath down on the billion-year-old batholith basalt banks of the famous Salmon River, which, much to my current mortification, I had signed up to float down. To make things worse, the Salmon also is called the River of No Return, which meant, of course, that I would never get out alive. I'd never return home, never see my dog again, my French china, the little black dress Tweeds finally got around to mailing me after it was back-ordered for three months . . . so much for a Cindy Crawford Christmas. I knew my whole life was going down that black snake hole with the great green river reptile that was, at the moment, still slithering past my feet. I cursed myself for putting myself through this.

"Need sun block?" asked an insufferably cheerful river guide.

"No," I replied. "I need a lobotomy."

We were putting in, as they say in the river running business, at Corn Creek, a two-hour drive from the already remote town of Salmon, Idaho. At the moment the place looked like an ant farm. Fat yellow rafts and elegant high-sided wooden dory boats waited in the shallows while troops of extremely tan people crawled all over them. They were our fleet of guides—one per guest, I noted—and their mission was to stash the mountains of supplies that littered the beach into secret compartments deep in the bowels of the vessels that would carry us downstream for the next six days. Coolers, tents, duffle bags, sleeping bags, tables, lanterns, cooking gear, rubber boots and backpacks . . . the scene looked to me like preparations for war.

"You can stow your ammo can here," offered a quiet dory guide named Lonnie Hutson. We had, indeed, been given genuine government issue metal ammo cans in which to keep the stuff we wanted near us at all times—sunglasses, cameras . . . arsenic. I studied the other guests for similar signs of angst. Nothing. Just smiles and spirited stomping around.

"Hi, I'm Jeanne," announced a pretty woman with an East Coast accent. "That's my husband, Herb." Herb waved and smiled, which made him look exactly like Lorne Greene. They were, it turned out, a bonanza—a psychologist and doctor team from Maryland who had already done O.A.R.S.'s seventeen-day Grand Canyon dory trip and lived to tell the tale . . . many times and with *great* enthusiasm. I asked Jeanne if I could ride in her lap.

That, of course, is all you have to say to a psychologist to get her undivided attention.

"This your first river trip?" she asked. I told her about the near-drowning, leaving out the stampeding buffalo and Outer Mongolia parts, and was relieved to see little spaniels of compassion dog paddle across her face. Jeanne patted my arm.

"Then, this is the best thing you can do for yourself," she said. "I was just as scared when we did the Grand Canyon, but by the end of the trip the white water was like an exciting friend and the walls of the canyon had become my home. Besides, these are the best guides in the world and this is the safest company—we researched it thoroughly before we chose it. You'll be fine."

"I'll be *damned*," I thought. I *was* damned, in fact. Lonnie had just given me a front row seat in the upcoming theater of disaster, pointing me to the bow of his dory.

"Keep your life preserver on at all times," he instructed. "And if you *do* go out of the boat, stay on your back and *keep your toes up*. And we'll come get you."

"Where?" I thought. "In China?" Even though it was high summer in a drought year and the water was stunningly low, the Salmon, as far as I could tell, was moving along at a serious clip.

How could someone in a boat behind someone in the water ever hope to catch up? I decided right then and there that I was *never, ever,* under *any* circumstances, going out of that boat. When we pushed off the bank at Corn Creek, I had a death grip on the gunwale with my left hand, my right fingers tourniqueted around the hand grip and my toes jammed under the bow hatch. I looked, I am sure, like Wile E. Coyote trying to hold back yet another Roadrunner boulder, but I didn't care. "Call me Ishmael," I thought. "Call me a chicken. Just *don't* call me a lifeguard because *this* sailor's staying dry come hell *and* high water."

Even from the depths of paranoid dementia I could see that the Salmon River is a beautiful place. It is, in fact, one of the longest undammed American rivers left. This triumph occurred largely due to the heroic efforts of a man named Frank Church and of former Idaho governor, Cecil D. Andrus, both of whom saw to it that the millions of acres of unspoiled wildlands through which we were now floating were kept that way. Idaho's glorious unfettered heart is now called the Frank Church River of No Return Wilderness. Bear, elk, eagle and bighorn sheep call it home. It is, indeed, a masterwork of rock and pine, river and sky, and very serious white water.

"What's that?" I asked Lonnie. It sounded like rolling thunder.

"That's our first serious white water," he said, "This is a drop and pool river," he added, as if abstract analysis could somehow derail the tsunami of panic that was flooding my mind.

I can now proudly say that I *personally* know how General Lee felt when he heard all those damn Yankees coming up over the draw. How Ralph Branca felt when he heard the crack of Bobby Thompson's bat at the 1951 World Series. How Beryl Markham felt when she heard her plane's engine sputter over Nova Scotia. How the itsy bitsy spider felt when it heard the first raindrops come down the water spout. Because I am now on a first-name basis with that sense of dread breaded with destiny that deep-fries your brain in two seconds flat. You know what's coming and you know there's not a damn thing you can do about it. History has been written in the grease stains of such events.

In my case, of course, the ordeal was more hysteric than historic. Or, rather, hairsteric. The guttural growl of the impending rapids triggered an instantaneous replay of my entire drowning experience, ponytail rescue and all. Adrenaline shot through my body. My hair hurt. I couldn't breathe so I held my breath . . . and assumed Wile E. Coyote Position.

Lonnie surveyed the roiling water calmly—you could almost see the physics and logarithms computing in his eyes. He rowed the dory to one side, then let the river do the rest. It did. Suddenly we were flying. Dipping and flying with water spraying out in all directions. Suddenly, my drowning memory was eclipsed by an earlier one, a thing of absolute delight. What was it? Boat. Speed. Water spray. Laughter! Happy squeals and laughter. My sisters. The Matterhorn. DISNEYLAND!!!!

There is a time before fear. A time of joy as pure as a bunch of kids running around chasing each other just to do it. A time when you feel in every cell of your body the miracle of your own existence. We are born into it, every one of us, and even though life with adults—and certainly *as* adults—tends to tarnish it, often badly, what I learned on the river that morning is that you can have it back.

"Lonnie," I said with tears in my eyes. "That was *fun*."

"That was Killum," he replied, smiling. "Killum Rapids."

"Kill 'em?" I repeated, and started to laugh. "Kill 'em Rapids!" I shrieked. For the rest of the trip, the rest of the rapids were a piece of birthday cake.

We were a flotilla of five—two dories and three support rafts—and a crew of ten—five guests and five guides, including a brawny young man named Colby Hawkinson who was in training and wasn't allowed to row live people. He was, however, entrusted with the beer, which I took as a supreme vote of confidence from the other guides. As for the guests, besides Jeanne and Herb there were Mike, a California businessman, and his beautiful, college-student daughter, Jenny. Like Jeanne and Herb, they, too, had been down the Colorado River. I was the only real river rookie of the bunch.

With the exception of Colby-the-trainee, our guides were all veterans. Curt Chang had actually founded what is now the Idaho dory arm of O.A.R.S. twenty years ago. Lonnie had been a river guide for seventeen years. The two junior guides, Don Rhoades and Brannon Riceci, had six and four years on the water respectively. The water, in fact, was the only real problem we had, give or take a few raging forest fires. It was lower than anybody had ever seen it. That meant rocks no one had ever navigated were now exposed, and riffles once floated over with ease were now shallow boat-busters. Everyone was worried about getting the dories down the river in one piece. It was going to be a bumpy ride. But first, lunch.

Besides safety and service, O.A.R.S. guides are famous for their cooking. I would add that they should be famous for their kitchens, which are astonishing feats of construction and deconstruction that remind you of the circus coming to town. Once Lonnie, the trip captain, selected a beach, the crew eviscerated the rafts, set up the cook station and had lunch ready before I had figured out how to undo my life jacket. Et, voila! We were in Lebanon. There on the sand beneath the pines we were served fresh hummus sandwiches, grilled eggplant and excellent tomato and cucumber salad. If they had trotted out Turkish coffee and fresh-baked baklava I wouldn't have been surprised. The guides' baking skills, as I later learned, definitely could have handled that fantasy.

The lunch kitchen vanished as quickly as it had appeared, and while kingfishers cruised the air above us, we embarked once more. The air above us, in fact, had become somewhat of an issue. It was an opalescent pink, the particle-rich gift of downstream forest fires. After Fear of Rapids, Fear of Smoke had been second on my list of concerns—either one could have made breathing equally uninviting. But even now, with a strong wind whipping down the canyon, the thick, heavy air was pleasant, like the aroma of a campfire. Floating through the forest itself, I was sure, would have been another story.

"You have to remember that this fire moves about a mile or two an hour," Lonnie explained. "You could out-walk it blindfolded."

That did it. My final fear was foiled. There was only one small, nagging concern left: la toilette.

"First, you have to remember to take your helmet," Lonnie began. We had made camp on a handsome beach, king salmon and Idaho steaks were already popping on the barbecue and our gear was neatly stowed in cute little igloo tents that kept threatening to turn into Eskimo yo-yos and go cartwheeling across the sand because we happened to be in the middle of a major windstorm. Nonetheless, it was time for Latrine Captain Lonnie to give his official Toilet Talk. So, we all stood in an attentive if squinting circle around him and a little, wooden-seated Sani-Can that looked suspiciously like the one that first coaxed you out of diapers.

Someone, probably Dr. Herb, asked if the helmet was for protecting you if the wind blew you off the throne.

"No," Lonnie replied. "It's so that other campers know if someone's using the head."

"That's using your head," offered Guide and Stand-up Comic Don Rhoades, who wasn't supposed to be at our talk in the first place. Lonnie delicately ignored him, explained that new toilet paper was in *this* can and used toilet paper went in *that* can, then he informed us that for both hygienic and ecological purposes we must "separate functions," as in do #1 in a plastic tub (fitted with a wooden seat) and #2 in the Sani-Can. There was a little hand-held plastic hospital-looking urinal thing for those who found this rule too physically challenging. Personally, I was beginning to wish I were still in diapers, but thought better of reporting this to Jeanne.

Once we were finished with the Sani-Can, we were to sprinkle the whole business with sweet-smelling lime powder kept in a former herb jar still labeled "Parsley"—a nice touch, I thought. Finally, we were obliged under penalty of Death by E. coli to *wash our hands* with the antiseptic liquid soap and water kept there.

All in all, it was an elegant system, clean, smart and very private. Once everyone left, I decided to try it out. Apart from ending up looking like George Washington thanks to the wind blowing a cloud of lime powder into my hair, I found my first Sani-Can experience, well, a relief. It also had the best view in camp, which, we soon learned, is the O.A.R.S. toilet tradition.

Dinner was wonderful, despite the wind. I mean salmon *and* steak? Fresh corn on the cob *and* spaghetti? How could they top that? They did . . . with homemade strawberry shortcake (Curt had baked the biscuits at home), fresh berries and whipped cream hand-whipped by Brannon in a metal bowl held *in* the river for proper chilling. It was as if the Camping Goddess had flown down on pine-scented wings and gone Zing!: "Thy white water fear shall turn to glee, thy forest fire smoke shall turn to incense, thy wilderness bathroom shall be beauteous and scenic and thou shalt be fed like Queen Piggy her Royal Self . . . we just threw the wind in so you wouldn't think you'd died and gone to heaven."

Actually, once I crawled into my sleeping bag I thought I *had* died . . . and gone nowhere. Talk about stiff! The pad for which I had paid a fortune felt maybe two degrees softer than your basic bedrock.

"You should have bought a Paco Pad," Colby said when I dragged myself to the campfire and complained. "They're the best."

"Instead she got a Snore-No-More," Don replied in a Monty Python soprano.

"A Sleep-Be-Gone," Colby added shrilly.

"A Comfort-Be-Damned," Brannon cried.

I crawled back into my tent and finally fell asleep listening to the lullaby of the wind and the sweet breathy song of the river . . . and Don shrieking to Brannon: "You have no arms or legs. I'm not going to fight you anymore." And Brannon screeching back: "Oh, it's only a flesh wound. . . . "

Breakfast was fresh blueberry pancakes, sausage and Lonnie's excellent coffee, which was so strong that morning that we pronounced it "Rodeo Brew." The wind had stilled, the day was bright and the sky was that Tidy-Bowl blue of those Don Ho cocktails you always end up not drinking in Honolulu. You start thinking tropical thoughts like that when you're floating along on a hot morning in big sky country . . . until you hear the distant growl of an approaching rapid. Salmon Falls.

Jenny and I rode in Brannon's dory that day—for variety, every day everyone switched guides—and Brannon looked concerned. To the left, water fanned over huge exposed boulders. To the right a narrow chute between two rock walls waited like a cavity in the devil's molar.

"That's the tightest I've ever seen it," Brannon said. "There's no margin for error."

We watched transfixed as Lonnie, carrying Jeanne, Herb and Mike, navigated the slot without a hitch. Brannon followed his lead and we made it through just fine.

"The rafts aren't gonna make it," he warned. "They're too fat."

Sure enough, Don's raft got stuck halfway. Lonnie and Brannon beached their dories, scrambled back over the rocks and leaped aboard. Then they all started jumping up and down like demented gorillas. I couldn't hear Don but I *knew* he was saying something like: "That's *my* banana . . . now give it back or I'll smash you with this paddle."

Suddenly, the raft lurched free and the rest of us cheered. We cheered again and again when Curt's and Colby's rafts made it through. By the time we arrived at Barth Hot Springs for lunch we were in a jovial mood, even though the weather had taken a turn for the worse and everyone was chilled. After a short hike, a rejuvenating communal soak and another stellar luncheon a la playa we pushed off again . . . and swiftly hit rock bottom. Literally. Blam! Blam, blam! The dory bounced off two barely disguised boulders then snagged on a third. Curt's raft pushed us free.

"We lived," Brannon announced.

"On the next one we might have to get out and wade," Lonnie hollered.

"What we need is the Flintstones' car with a little hole in the bottom," Brannon replied.

By now, the low water made navigation so tricky Lonnie insisted on checking out all rapids before taking them. So, we would pull over and tie up to a rock. Then the guides would hike downstream, squat like Native-American scouts and discuss the water for about twenty minutes.

"Does this one have a name?" I heard Brannon ask.

"Naw," Lonnie replied. "It's just tight. It'll be hard to be clean on it," he said finally. "You've got permission to bang 'em." And so we did.

For one particularly shallow rapid Lonnie had Jenny and me transfer to Colby's raft. With less weight dories do better in such situations, and being rubber, rafts tend to thwang off rocks, rather than plow into them. So, we had an opportunity to experience why rafts are a lot like shampoo—they give your ride more body and bounce, and make it more manageable. Rafts will, in fact, practically wash your hair for you. Because, without the protective high sides of a dory, you get a lot wetter. In fact, it was on that little raft sojourn that I was able to personally experience what I like to call "The Ice Bra," wherein a five-foot column of icy water leaps out of the river unannounced and dives straight down your shirt. That was the last time I rafted without zipping my jacket up to my nose.

By the time we made camp that evening we all felt as battered as the poor dories. But Lonnie had chosen a beautiful spot called Swimmer's Beach. Chipmunks scolded us from the boulders there, a mink dodged out of sight and a family of river otters paddled by like a very nervous welcoming committee.

"I feel like a kid at summer camp," I announced.

"You are," Lonnie replied.

But no summer camp I ever knew dished up the kind of supper we had that night: Colby's excellent barbecued chicken with rice to absorb the heavenly sauce, Greek salad with green *and* kalamata olives . . . and fresh baked brownies. There was a wild game of horseshoes after dinner, then Jenny told about five million ghost stories, then Don, Brannon and Colby had a coal tossing contest . . . barehanded, a sport which rendered their complaints of "rowing blisters" the next day somewhat suspect.

Fun aside, it was a marvelous night, filled with aromatic zephyrs, cricket music and the haunted cries of the night birds on their evening hunt. Never had the evening sky seemed fairer. Never had the stars shone brighter. Never had I wished more that I hadn't been such a big chicken and arranged to bail out of this trip two days early. That was *before* my white water epiphany, of course, but arrangements had been made, the plane was hired, and, like going down a rapid, once you're committed there's no getting out of it. And there wasn't. I couldn't remember feeling so blue.

"Tomorrow's my last day," I confessed to Jeanne. She understood, of course, and was so sympathetic that just to make me feel better she made the quintessential Girl Camper sacrifice: She gave me some of her Baby Wipes.

It was a grand day, that last one. First we had breakfast with a family of seven bighorn sheep who marched through the far edge of camp to take a drink in the river. Then we got to go down Big Mallard, rapids so colossal that Curt told everyone to "batten down the hatches."

"We be battened," Brannon answered.

"We're battin' a thousand," Don concurred.

We were. Everyone made it through this tricky white water just fine. As well as Elkhorn, Growler and Ludwig, famous Salmon River rapids, all. That afternoon we made camp beneath a bridge on the far side of an old homestead called Jim Moore's. Black bear were feasting in his orchard, as their little hills of oxidized apple scat testified. Colby informed us that, acting as a miner's general store, Moore's place had been quite a going affair during the gold rush.

"Before he died in 1942, he supposedly buried his life savings somewhere on the property," Colby said.

"What if I found it?" Herb asked.

"You do and we split it, buddy," Lonnie commanded. "I got you this far."

Don, Brannon and Lonnie cooked that night and dinner was perfect again: caesar salad, fettucini with fresh shrimp and red and yellow peppers, and Lonnie's amazing fresh cod with bouquets of fresh dill and lemon wheels. It started raining midway, and everyone helped erect a cooking tarp. Then Brannon vanished and reappeared wearing a chrome yellow rain hat that looked like "The Flying Nun Goes Deep Sea Fishing."

"I can't cook with someone wearing that," Don complained.

"You got a problem with this hat?" Brannon replied. "I got no problem with this hat. The hat stays." It did. And the only thing better that night was Curt's peach cobbler, baked in a Dutch oven right on the campfire.

It was hard to leave the next morning. Besides feeling like a giant chicken-dweeb, I knew I'd miss everyone terribly. We all hugged and exchanged addresses, then Curt rowed me downriver one hour to the pickup spot. When my plane headed back up river I pasted my eyes to the window until I found our camp . . . then began waving like an idiot. No one could see me up that high, but I kept waving anyway. Then I saw her. A little white dot waving back as wildly as I was. Jeanne! Tears threw themselves voluntarily down my unwashed cheeks. Jeanne! Jeanne! Good-bye! Bye! Thanks for the Baby Wipes!!! Bye!

All that stuff you hear about the deep bonding that occurs on wilderness trips is true—especially if you share Baby Wipes. Without all the complications of home, the experience is an act of purity. And you remember it that way. Pure terror. Pure joy. Pure air, sky and river. Pure friendship. The scary parts are really scary, the triumphs true. You rely on the experienced wisdom of your guides to get you through—the rest is your own courage. When it comes to adventure, I've come to believe in a motto that's a little twist on a great, old Beatles line: The risk you take is equal to the growth you make.

Looking down at the river from the plane that day it reminded me of a piece of beautiful dark music, broken at graceful intervals by the white notes of the rapids. An oboe solo, an aural cascade, bridging one piece of the melody to another until, together, they sing the glorious, bittersweet song of the last free-flowing river in America.

The Whole
Wide World

Into the Mystic: Ireland

There were three of us: Lucy Brown, me and Lucy Brown's hair, which hangs down her back like four feet of silken sheet metal. It is, we reckoned, about seven years old, and like all seven-year-olds, it has a boundless capacity for making friends, reaching out in all directions, wrapping its tiny fingers around the arms of perfect strangers, flight attendants, my lunch. It is a mixed blessing to fly 6,000 miles with such a companion. Near the end of the flight Lucy sent her hair to its room, gathering it into a quiet place at the back of her neck and allowing me, for the first time, to see out the plane window. There beneath us, boiling like slate stew, was the Irish Sea. Just beyond that, reaching toward America, the green geometry of its farms spreading out like a flat, faceted emerald, was the dear and dangerous country of Ireland.

The moment we stepped off the plane we learned that Ireland is a place of the elements. It does not snap a movable metal hallway onto the door of your plane to deliver you from one artificial environment into another without so much as a whiff of where you've just landed. When you get off the plane in Dublin, you get off into the wind. And it was at this point that Lucy's hair decided to go home. It quickly turned to get back on the airplane, blinding me in the process so that I did not see the smoky figure waiting for us just inside the airport door.

"Philip!" Lucy yelled.

There he was. In all his rumpled Irish glory. A fine wool tweed suit that hadn't been pressed in a couple of years, a somewhat baffled tie and elegantly scuffed shoes, pink cheeks, sad moon eyes and black hair that obviously would rather have stayed in bed. He looked like a cross between Robert Mitchum and an owl.

He is, in fact, an architect. During her previous European tour, Lucy, an artist and graphic designer, had helped Philip with some last-minute architecture assignments in London and they became fast friends. They also became sort of transcontinental soul mates, mainly because Lucy is a collector of all things strange and artful, and Philip is one of Ireland's more entertaining specimens.

"I got your letter," he said in a tone that seemed not only to explain his presence at the airport at that particular moment, but the very existence of time, space and the universe itself. It was difficult to decide if Philip operated in an extremely high state of consciousness or was simply from another planet, but whatever it was it infused the air around him with some sort of unintentional mystery, and when he suggested tea, Lucy and I agreed with near silly enthusiasm. We soon found ourselves in a car that matched Philip's suit, zipping through Dublin's kamikaze traffic toward something or someone called Bewley's.

"Jersey milk from our own farms," the sign read. The milk was yellow with cream. "Irish brown bread," read another. The slices were thick with oats and wheat. To the back of the building, bevies of women in brown uniforms floated in and out of the steam of some sort of colossal tea-making machine. And the place rang with the porcelain music of happy restaurants.

Bewley's was the most ancient cafeteria Lucy or I had ever seen. All of its parts were framed in dark wood and there was a kind of film over everything. It reminded me of the kitchens of Gulf of Mexico towns, where the atmosphere is laminated with the grease of a thousand fried shrimp and salted humidity. At Bewley's the atmosphere was more bacon fat and tea steam, but the feeling was the same: These are places built by and for the people who live there. Things are simply kept comfortable. And for those of us who live in the cold heart of American quick-change artistry, this is a major blessing. Muscle by muscle, nerve by nerve, we felt ourselves relax.

Between Bewley's balm and basic jet lag, we were practically in a deep trance by the time Philip dropped us off at our hotel. My mind at that point felt like it had spent the last five nights in a pub. All I could remember was that Philip was picking us up again at eight that night and something about Ireland having "done away with animal glue," which I hoped had something to do with buying postcard stamps.

If it can be arranged, one should always tour a new city with an architect. If it can also be arranged, the tour should be conducted during the daytime. Now, Philip is an excellent tour guide; like all good architects, he knows the important buildings by heart, which he dutifully pointed out to us one by one, but since it was dark we couldn't see anything. However, our overall impression was this: Dublin is in a rather deplorable state of decay due to the decline of the Irish pound, inflation, unemployment, lack of import commodities, the price of Guinness. It is, however, also experiencing a structural renaissance, and in the quiet darkness spinning by our car window, piles of 200-year-old bricks and glass sat patiently beside gloriously refurbished historic monuments with newly polished brass doorknockers and brightly painted windowpanes. It was with this sense of restoration that we arrived at a club called Baggots, which Philip himself had recently re-designed, to hear one of the most innovative and beloved rock bands in Ireland, Moving Hearts.

Philip knew half the people there, including Tony, the owner, who is considered the "Pita Bread King" of Dublin, and, true to form, he instantly handed us a couple of overweight pita sand-wiches exploding with sprouts and veggies.

Before Lucy and I could digest the significance of eating such utterly California cuisine for our first Irish supper, Moving Hearts moved. Rather they began to breathe, since their songs congregate around the strange, windy instruments of traditional Irish music. Uilleann pipes and low whistles came to life in high-pitched cadences. A bodhran drum created the heartbeat, and a bouzouki wove a string netting around the whole thing with me-tallic, mandolinlike grace. Suddenly everyone was on their feet. All around us people were bouncing. This was rock and roll?

It was more of a jig. Then a synthesizer took over and an elec-tric bass added a mean undertow and almost imperceptibly the jig slid into jazz. And we began to understand. This was something new. It carried with it the raw force of synthesis and supersedure, of colliding cultures and agreement. We decided right there it could only be called Irish fusion.

∼

When you think about shopping in Ireland, you usually think about buying Irish linen and Irish crystal and Irish whiskey and those wonderful big hand-knit Irish woolen sweaters. What you don't think about is that Ireland is part of Europe and therefore is privy to European fashion. And since the pound was worth about two and a half times less than it was when I was in Europe ten years ago, Lucy and I found that we could buy Italian boots and French dresses for the price of American polyester sweatshirts. And that is exactly what we did the next morning while Philip finished up some work.

As Irish as it is, Dublin remains the cosmopolitan city of Ireland. There are streets and streets of boutiques and good department stores in the heart of the commercial district. But the best part is that it's all so walkable. Everybody walks and shops in Dublin. And even though Dublin is a big city and all big cities take their toll on the human psyche, even though times are tough and people's faces are often policed by private pain as they tense their bodies against the cold, they're all in this together and they know it. You can feel it on the streets. The purpose and strength of it is contagious. It makes you feel powerful. It makes you defiant. It made Lucy and me take enormous fashion risks: Lucy bought some flat, round-toed shoes that were as green as the Irish countryside; I bought a Danish jumpsuit with an unusually large belt that gave me a sort of Celtic warrior look. Luckily, just before we started resembling a two-woman chorus line for Boy George, it was time to meet Philip back at the hotel.

Philip does not live in Dublin. He lives in a sweet little farmhouse about twenty miles south of Dublin in County Wicklow, one of the loveliest regions of mountain and lake in Ireland.

Philip led and we followed in our silver, rented "Dan Dooley Knock-Along" Toyota. Like the English, the Irish drive on the wrong side of the road. They also have their steering wheels and gear shifts on the wrong side of the car. Since I was born with what I call directional dyslexia—that is, I get my right and left mixed up even at home—I figured it would be far safer if Lucy drove. But that was before I realized that the front seat passenger sat face-to-face with the oncoming traffic, and since Lucy was used to driving on the other side, she tended to cut it a little close. She was also trying to follow Philip, whose driving motto seemed to be "born to die," so I cannot say that the journey out of Dublin and into Wicklow was particularly educational. It was, however, a regular Nautilus workout for my knuckles, and once we found ourselves surrounded by the rich and muscular landscape of the Wicklow valley, it was merely a matter of scraping me off the ceiling so I could get out and have a better view.

"These are the featherbeds," Philip yelled into the wind.

I looked around thankfully for a place to lie down, but there were only great, sloping slabs of land that, at certain intervals, had been curiously cut away to reveal the blackest earth I had ever seen.

"That's turf," Philip cried. "What we use in the fire."

Pointing to a big nub of a mountain way off in the distance, he added, "That's Sugarloaf. And this is gorse." He plucked a valiant little yellow flower from a low, wind-battered plant. Then, to my horror, Philip squished the flower between his fingers and stuck it under my nose, and to my astonishment it smelled just like coconut.

"It smells like coconut," I said.

"Yes," he replied and returned to his car.

Lucy was glad to follow suit, having spent the last five minutes chasing her hair, which was chasing itself all over the place in a frantic attempt to get back into the car. And we were off again.

The Wicklow valley is actually one of Ireland's geographic treasures. It has, for instance, the greatest granitelands in the British Isles—made of molten and angry rock that rose from the viscera of the earth about 500 million years ago and put a permanent kink in the neck of the valley's thick, slatey upper crust. The wicked Wicklow wind further assaulted the poor slate until its health failed altogether. Its powdery remains are now scattered at the feet of its predecessors, the victorious granite mountains of County Wicklow.

It is, perhaps, the ossified influence of this post-Paleolithic panorama that makes Wicklow residents so hardheaded. No sooner had we driven a scant quarter mile than Philip pulled over again, this time to point out an old stone structure down the hill to the left.

"It's a reform school," he explained. "Run by a young couple. That's where they put the bad boys of Belfast."

Belfast.

How was I to write about Ireland without mention of the northern part of the island? The chicken-livered part of me that couldn't handle driving in Dublin wasn't about to risk its life over incurable religious mania. But my mercilessly macabre, maddeningly curious, black cat streak—which led me to writing in the first place—purred. I tried to give the cat some coconut gorse to play with, but it was no use. Visions of intrigue and obsession seduced my brain, and the gorse blossom fell back into the brittle nest of bracken and bog.

The hills around Philip's house have, if Ireland will forgive me, that lolling beauty of a New Zealand travel poster. They are, however, latticed with decidedly Irish stone fences made hundreds of years ago with the stones gathered when the land was originally cleared. The reason they haven't fallen down yet is that they were stacked with spaces between them—a sort of stone crochet—so that the wind could get through. From a distance the fences look like draped necklaces that surround square, white-washed farmhouses, set jewel-like and apart on the green throat of the land.

It is a vista of extravagant beauty. But you have only to lift your eyes to see a sight that easily makes you forget to breathe: the Wicklow cloudworks.

Their velocity is phenomenal, their antics endless. Huge and luminous, they tumble like cauliflowers boiling in the bluest of soups.

Philip shares his rented 300-year-old, three-bedroom farmhouse with Cyril, an award-winning photojournalist. And they share it with all their friends, young people like them, mostly in their thirties and college educated, who work in Dublin but live, on principle, in the country. They move freely, stopping by for tea, dropping in for dinner, borrowing tools, bringing by a new album, in a way that quickly flushed out Lucy's and my own American territoriality. We are far more distanced than they are, even from our close friends. We draw much clearer lines between ourselves, our possessions, our time, our space, our futures. After living one week among Philip's friends, I was convinced that we are suffering terribly from what can only be called a loss of tribe.

You never know who you're going to have breakfast with at Philip's, and when we walked downstairs that first morning, two strangers were having tea at the kitchen table. One was a carrot-haired man, the other was a tall woman with an Irish accent that rivaled any we'd heard so far. It was a delicate thing that rose at the end of each sentence like a question, and her pronunciation was strangely soft. She would, for instance, say "th" as a "d" or a "t," so that "the" came out as "da" and "thing" sounded like "ting."

Lucy and I made our somewhat self-conscious entrance.

"Ah, the enlightened women," the man said. " And should I be afraid of you?" He smiled a crinkly smile and dutifully poured us each a cup of tea, one of which was intercepted by Cyril, who had just cruised through the kitchen like a fast-motion Groucho Marx.

"Breakfast for four? Oh, eggsellant," he said in a voice that sounded like a cross between a horse's neigh and Grandma Moses. "Would you have an egg? Or will it be porridge now?"

"Sounds like you're on your last eggs, mate," the red-haired man said.

"And you can go to shell, you can," Cyril replied, and plugged in the electric kettle for more tea. Then he disappeared into the living room, and in a few moments the most joyful Irish music filled the house.

"What is that?" Lucy asked.

"Why, it's the 'Song for Ireland,' it 'tis, it 'tis," Cyril said, "and a mighty tune, that, a might-tee tune."

"It's by De Danann," the woman explained. "They're a favorite traditional Irish band."

"Don't you think you should introduce us," the man said to Cyril, who was now poking pieces of black peat into the wood-burning kitchen stove. They filled the house with a delicious burnt-leaves scent that clung to our sweaters like Irish perfume.

Cyril whipped around and, with a courtly bow, he said,

"Grainne, Lucy, Barry, Lucy, Grainne, Jessie, Barry, Jessie, have another cup of tea?"

"Well, it has to be made with completely boiling water," said the man, who seemed to be named Barry.

"Aughk, bother!" said Cyril.

"You're going to learn something here, Cyril. Tea must be made with boiling water. Coffee must be made at just under boiling water."

"And tea goes much better with Irish brown bread," Lucy added.

"Are we out?" Cyril asked with extreme mortification. "Just a minute, then," and he really did begin to neigh like a horse and make running hoof sounds across the kitchen floor.

"Would you like some hoof and hoof in your tea?" asked Barry.

"Oh, Barry, they just woke up," laughed Grainne.

The music from the living room spun into a spirited jig, and Lucy asked Cyril, "How do you dance to this?"

"You'll see when we get to Galway," replied Philip, who had just slinked into the kitchen, his hair still wet from a bath.

"There are jigs and reels," Barry said. "Cyril, what's the difference between a jig and a reel?"

"On one you catch trout, on the other you catch salmon."

"That reminds me," said Philip. "Maybe we should take you to the Aran Islands to dance."

"No, they'd be taken off the floor," Barry replied.

"What floor?" I asked.

"There would be strange men with big arms and big hands and they dance with these girls and just lift them off the floor," he said and flew an imaginary partner above our heads.

"Yeah, they don't know their own strength," Philip explained. "They're all fishermen. They row all the time."

"Yes, they do have a lot of rows," Cyril added.

"Sometimes they have salmon roe," Barry added.

Grainne rolled her eyes.

"Yes, they don't know their own strength and, of course, they mightn't be the full shilling either."

"Do you mean they might not be playing with a full deck?" Lucy asked.

"Eggsactly," Barry replied.

And so it was decided that we should go to Galway on the west coast of Ireland. And it was decided that Philip would go with us, if we could wait a few days for him to finish a project. It was also decided that Cyril and Philip were late for work and Grainne and Barry would take us for a drive around Wicklow that morning. But not before Grainne went home to take some soup off the stove. Lucy went upstairs to brush her teeth, I poured another cup of tea, and Barry began thumbing through a book I'd left on the table the night before.

"*The Tao of Pooh?*" he said. "So Winnie-the-Pooh's a Taoist? Now that's interesting. Do you think he is?"

"Well," I began slowly, "the author, Benjamin Hoff, thinks that Pooh is a, well, a Western Taoist master."

Barry opened the book and started reading out loud from the preface:

> "What's that?" the Unbeliever asked.
>
> "Wisdom from a Western Taoist," I said.
>
> "It sounds like something from *Winnie-the-Pooh*," he said.
>
> "It is," I said.
>
> "That's not about Taoism," he said. . . . "It's about this dumpy little bear that wanders around asking silly questions, and making up songs, and going through all kinds of adventures, without ever accumulating any amount of intellectual knowledge or losing his simpleminded sort of happiness. *That's* what it's about. . . . "
>
> "Same thing," I said.

Barry laughed. "That's why I left Trinity and went to Peru," he said.

"Trinity College?" I asked.

"Trinity College," Barry replied. "In Dublin. I was a math professor there."

"So what are you doing now?" I asked.

"Whatever needs doing," he replied.

"And where do you stay?"

"Wherever I can."

"Should I take the camera?" asked Lucy, who had just come down the stairs in a cloud of spearmint toothpaste. I was pleased to see that her hair was contained in two neat braids. Grainne arrived moments later, and we all piled into our silver Toyota Knock-Along.

Lucy turned on the radio and a news broadcast came on—in Gaelic. It sounded like a cross between German and Hawaiian.

"Did you all study Gaelic in school?" I asked.

"Well, I could have," Barry replied, "but I'm from the Dark North, you see. British occupation."

The Dark North. The cat's tail twitched.

"What city?" I asked.

"Belfast," he said.

Belfast. The cat pounced.

"Barry . . . "

For the first time, Barry's smile faded and an almost painful weariness replaced it.

"I don't like to talk about it," he said. Then he looked at me and he took a deep breath.

"Okay," he said, like an old man who had just agreed to let a dentist pull all his teeth.

"If you were to drive up from Dublin to Belfast, you would cross the border just after Dundalk and into a town called Newry.

And at the border you will generally notice a lot of British Army land rovers, jeeps and small armored cars or what they call armored personnel carriers, and going through the center of Newry, you will notice that the police stations and public buildings have wire grilles all round them and are all fenced off, and this is to stop people from throwing petrol bombs into them. Sometimes the buildings will be inside a huge, metal box. This is to stop people from shooting into them.

"Then as you go past Newry, you go onto an actual motorway, like a freeway, which brings you into Belfast. And when you arrive at Belfast, the first thing you'll probably see is smoke. It's kind of a dirty city. But if you're to go into the center of the town, at some point you have to pass through a security gate in order to get into the shopping area. And the people have got kind of used to this business of being searched every time they go into town.

"Now you can do a little tour and go off into places like Bally Murphy and the Falls Road, which are the Catholic ghettos and are in terrible condition. They're a shambles, a lot of homes have been burned down. There are few facilities. Then the Protestant side of things is the Shankill Road, which is a couple of streets away and looks very similar. And between the Falls and the Shankill, there's what they call a Peace Line, which is a long, huge wall that they built all the way along between the two.

"And most of the people go on about their business and it

is possible to lead quite a normal life and the only real inconvenience would be the fact that your car may be stopped and searched at any time, or you may personally be searched by the British Army or the police or what they call the UDR, which is the Ulster Defense Regiment, a part of the British Army based in Northern Ireland.

"Most people can go up and stay a week or two quite safely because they'd always be taken out by people who know where they should and shouldn't go.

"The most dangerous places are the border towns, which are villages that are very strongly one way or the other, and all you'd need to do, as they say up there, is kick with the wrong foot in the wrong town."

Barry leaned back against the seat and lit a cigarette.

"You know, it's supposed to be a revolutionary struggle type thing, or a struggle for a united Ireland, but it has turned into a sectarian shoot-out between the IRA and the Protestant organizations, and that's all there is to it."

"Turn down there," Grainne said suddenly, and we found ourselves heading downhill toward what looked like a park beneath a mountain. In its middle was a huge brown lake.

County Wicklow is known for its lakes, which filled up with water after the glaciers scooped holes out of solid rock like so much granite ice cream. This one, Grainne informed us, belonged to Garrett Brown, a member of the Guinness family.

"I talked to him all afternoon once," Grainne said. "He's got a lot of wild stories and all that crack."

We parked by the brown lake and walked over to its shore and just when I was going to ask Grainne if it was full of Guinness, Barry started splashing around in his rubber boots. "These are called Wellingtons, you know," he said. Then he began to sing:

> *Oh, Wellies they are wonderful.*
> *Wellies they are swell.*
> *'Cause they keep out the water*
> *And they keep in the smell.*
> *And if you're in a room of folk*
> *You can always tell*
> *When someone takes off their Wellies.*

"By George," Lucy said. "I think we've found our Irish Pooh!"

"Yes!" I agreed. "And we'll have to call him Beary."

We were on the road again, high above the estate and all around us were coarse, mauve-colored bushes.

"That's all heather," said Grainne, one of the best bog guides around. "And those are Irish blueberries. They're called frockens. And there's some bog cotton. And you see how all the water here is tea-colored? Well, that's because of the tannin, sort of a bog tea, you could say."

It was getting dark. On the way back we stopped and bought things for dinner, which was a good lesson in Irish imports. There were red yams from Egypt, green beans from Kenya, cabbages from Holland and fennel root from France. There were also, Lucy and I noted, bottles of Mr. Clean, which, in Ireland, is called "Mr. Proper," some heavy-duty cleanser called "Gumption" and little cubes of beef bouillon called "Oxo," guaranteed to have "more man appeal."

Everyone showed up for dinner that night: Barry and Grainne, Philip and Cyril, Lucy and me, and we discussed our trip to Galway. Philip decided that we ought to overnight at his parents' cabin on Lough Conn in County Mayo, just north of Galway. There was a reason for this: Philip had become disenchanted with the life of an architect and was seriously considering the advantages of a life as either a musician or a furniture maker. He had already begun to collect flutes and whistles and odd pieces of wood, and there was an elderly furniture maker in County Sligo, not too far from the cabin, whom he wanted to visit.

That night, as Lucy and I wrapped ourselves around our hot water bottles, the wicked Wicklow wind whipped up a mournful lullaby, and from somewhere in the night we heard Philip answer with a wheezy, uncertain Irish melody on his new tin whistle.

After a breakfast of porridge, sausages, bacon and tea, we took off in a northwesterly direction. Lucy drove, Philip navigated, I prayed and Barry went along for the ride. Eventually we crossed the Shannon River, which ran right across the road. It's a boggy thing, full of estuaries and reedy weeds, and in every little river town we passed, the schoolchildren had their Wellies on.

John Surlis lives with his wife in a simple house in a village called Ballaghaderreen. All his life, he had made his living making one thing: the Irish kitchen chair.

Philip had brought him some apple wood. He hoped to get a lesson in exchange and he did. Mr. Surlis walked from behind the counter of his little store into his icy workshop and sat down on a benchlike contraption called a gray mare. His chickens watched him through the window.

"We have six or seven generations of furniture men in the family," he said. "We can trace it back 150 years."

He clamped a stick into the wooden jaws of the gray mare and began to work it with an old metal plane that almost looked cruel in his arthritic fingers.

Scrape. Scrape. Turn. Scrape. Scrape. Turn.

"I used to make everything in wood. Them tubs there. Milk churns. We made the ones that brought the butter to England in olden times."

Scrape. Scrape. Turn. Scrape. Scrape. Turn.

"We made the cradle. The old-time coffin. Some of my chairs even went to California."

Slowly, slowly, the stick moved in his hands. Slowly, it became a perfect chair leg. It was like watching a magic trick performed with such exaggerated deliberation you couldn't be sure it was happening at all. I loved the inherent peace of it. This, I thought, is a man who knows how to live.

Before we left, Mr. Surlis asked us to guess his age, and Lucy did.

"Eighty-one," she said.

"I'll be eighty-two this year."

"And what," I asked, "is the secret of your long life?"

John Surlis didn't hesitate.

"Work hard," he replied, "and never pretend you're getting old."

Philip's family cottage, on the shore of Lough Conn, is next to a secret all-night pub. The night we were there was special because it was the last night that Sean Kane would own it.

There was a furious turf fire going, and the local folk were gathered around it. Ireland's blood-chilling climate does that to people; they need the fire of alcohol and cigarettes, of pink salmon and red meat, of fast music and breathing bodies, just to keep warm.

For hours we drank Guinness and laughed and met people's relatives and watched the police chief get drunker and drunker until he was jumping over the bar to help Sean pull pints. When we finally made our way back outside and staggered up to the cabin, Philip suddenly leaned over and, grinning his otherworldly grin, said, "Sean says he can get us some poitin."

Sure enough, the bottle was delivered to our door the next morning, wrapped in newspaper.

Poitin is homemade Irish potato moonshine, and rumor has it that a bad batch can blind you, although neither Barry nor Philip knew anyone who'd actually been blinded. There is, however, what is known as the milk test, wherein you drip a drop of poitin into a plate of milk and watch closely. If it curdles around the edges, it's bad stuff. Ours didn't curdle. But it sent such powerful shock waves across the surface of the milk that I was still filled with apprehension.

Barry and Philip drank theirs straight. Lucy sipped hers carefully. I wouldn't drink any at all, until Barry made me a poitin toddy with lemon and honey, which tasted like warm vodka.

After our morning cocktail, we repacked the car and headed down the road to Galway. We made several stops on the way. One was at Philip's favorite deserted castle, which featured a twisted spine of a spiral stone staircase that rose straight up four stories and deposited us at the threshold of a missing wall, which offered a thrilling view of the green, green flatlands of western Ireland.

"The teddy bear's paws," Philip said.

"What?" I asked.

"The teddy bear's paws," he repeated. "You know, if you look on a map, Ireland looks like a teddy bear reaching toward America. The paws are County Mayo."

"And his brain's Northern Ireland?" Barry asked with a raised eyebrow.

"And Dublin's on his back," Philip laughed.

"And Belfast is on his neck, where he gets his ire up," Barry added.

"Or his IRA," Lucy added.

They each took a swig of poitin. Down below, a horse rolled in the mud.

The other stop we made was for cigarettes in a shop called Dunny's in the tiny village of Finny, or it might have been the shop called Finny's in the tiny village of Dunny. Poitin does that to you.

The rest of the drive to Galway belonged to Van Morrison and the Irish Paintbox Goddess. While his passionate "Into the Mystic" rolled out of the radio, colors rushed and blurred around our car windows. Toasted colors. Treacle colors. Mauve and hay, chartreuse and cream. Peach dust, burnt rose, powdered tea, pale lizard. And every so often, a dear little Irish farmhouse nestled into this renegade rainbow like a blank space on the canvas.

By the time we reached Galway, the goddess had painted the day blue. It's a seacoast town, full of the cool vapors of the wild Atlantic. But it is cozy and small, just like Freddie's house, which served as our home base for the whole visit.

Freddie is a marine biologist and very Irish. She is tough and sweet, independent and knows how to be a very good friend. It was Freddie who took us to the best sweater shop in Ireland.

It was run by a plump woman with rude red lipstick painted far above and beyond her lips, and a strange, shrill voice that was forever chattering to the handful of motley men who seemed to just hang around the shop and stare at things.

"They're a bit daft," Freddie warned us. "And prepare yourself for the odor."

We were not prepared. Apparently the owner's dogs and ensuing puppies were given free rein of the place without a convenient exit to the great outdoors. Lucy and I bravely complimented the cute puppies, raved about the stock and were invited to sort through the warehouse of hand-knit Irish woolen sweaters.

There was another communal supper that night at Freddie's, with the usual coming and going of old pals.

After dinner Freddie piled us into the old Knock-Along and we drove to a pub famous for its "sessions." Musicians from all around came with their fiddles and whistles and pipes and flutes and beautiful, clear voices and played nonstop while the rest of us pushed in around them like ants around sugar.

The party did not stop when the pub closed. It simply moved to the youth hostel across the street. And that's where the dancing began.

The musicians realigned themselves and squares of couples began to form. A jig exploded from the fiddles and the couples began to jump, making an enormous, rhythmic racket with the heels of their shoes.

"That's called battering," Freddie explained.

Lucy, Philip, Barry and I decided to try it, but between the poitin and a distinct lack of skill, we ended up sounding more like a stampede. Then Philip started dancing with Barry, Fred-Astaire-style, his cape flying. Barry handed Philip to Lucy and her hair, which had already started dancing behind her back. Then he slid over to me and, together, we did a dumpy little jig around the room.

Twelve
Flew
into the
Cuckoo's Nest:
Outer Mongolia

They were supposed to be seven feet long and weigh two hundred pounds. They were supposed to be the biggest salmon in the world and nobody had ever fished them but us . . . so where the hell were they?

First of all, you have to belong to the Fishermen's Order of Obsessed Lunatics or you would never do this to yourself. Only a F.O.O.L. would fly fourteen hours across the Pacific on a falling-apart plane with three hundred people who never turn off their reading lights, ride thirty-seven hours across the Gobi Desert in a sandstorm on a train that never stops doing the Jerk and drive twelve hours across the steppes of Outer Mongolia in a 1963 Soviet bus without shocks . . . just to catch a damn fish.

Like the other eleven fishing fools in our party, I wanted to break the world's record for a salmon taken on a fly. Since Mongolian taimen salmon supposedly weigh up to two hundred pounds, they definitely rate as the biggest on earth, the gonzo gift of the last Last Frontier.

The proper name of the big boys we were after was originally a Carmen Miranda dance tune called "Hucho hucho taimen," "hucho" rhyming with "mucho" and "taimen" rhyming with "amen," as in, "It's going to take mucho amen to catch these guys." They are native to Mongolia, China and Siberia, though Russian taimen have nearly been fished out. Their Mongolian brethren, on the other hand, have for the last ten thousand years swum free in great thawunking numbers because, as our American outfitter had gleefully informed us, "Mongolians don't fish," a fact that swiftly engendered Mongolian Mystery #1: Just what *were* those deeply rutted paths leading to every good fishing hole?

Scientifically, the genus *Hucho* is part of the salmonoid family, making *Hucho hucho* taimen officially a salmon. But I had my doubts. I come from serious salmon country, the American Northwest, where our platinum-flanked warriors leave the rivers of their birth as mere fingerlings, then spend four, sometimes six years cruising around the North Pacific, dodging killer whales and mile-long ghost nets until their bio-alarms set them on a crash course for home. Nothing, but *nothing*, fights like a Pacific king salmon hooked en route to the spawn, especially on light tackle. I have, for instance, personally witnessed a forty-nine-pound king salmon do red and silver cartwheels until it vanished down the cold back of Alaska's Kenai River, and I have had my rowboat towed half a mile up the Inside Passage by a twenty-eight-pounder that inspired a new T-shirt slogan: "Spawn 'Til You Die . . . or Die Trying."

But these local *Hucho hucho* dudes sounded like loiterers at best. The rivers they inhabit all drain into Siberia's big, flat Lake Baikal, not some great wild sea. Mongolian salmon make no distinguished journeys. They don't tick like an erotic time bomb, and they don't ride into town, hides ablazing, on the amber hem of every autumn. In short, they're frauds. Armchair adventurers who'd rather sink than swim and simply hang out in their respective rivers like Jabba the Hutt, going nowhere, taking no chances and getting as big as boats, their one redeeming and embarrassingly magnetic sporting quality. Unfortunately, it was late June and the rivers of northern Mongolia were too big and muddy to fish.

So there we were, the two scientists in the party and I,

alarmingly close to the Siberian border, groin-deep in the swollen Hongoi River, examining the squirming contents of the gill net the guides had set hours earlier, while a gray cashmere sweater of a sky unraveled above our heads. At the moment, it was the only kind of fishing you could do.

Biologists Frank Haw of Washington state, and Ed Brothers from New York, were just as determined as everyone else to set a new record for the world's largest salmon, which, at the moment, was held by a ninety-seven-pound king taken off the Kenai Peninsula. Stellar fly-fishermen both, they were also hard set on breaking the world's salmon-on-a-fly record. But, being scientists, they were just as determined to discover new species of fish. Mongolia, apparently, has one of the most underexplored fish fauna on earth, and it was still possible to ferret out some uncharted guppy there and maybe even name it after one's former girlfriend, as a pal of Brothers had done in Belize. On the off-chance of this minor scientific miracle, Dr. Brothers had lugged two five-gallon tubs of formaldehyde 6,000 miles across two continents and four countries, much to the annoyance of Chinese and Mongolian customs officers, who kept accusing him of trying to smuggle in American soy sauce.

Our fish camp, what there was of it, bustled with inactivity on the bank above us. Rogue Atlanta attorney George Polatty, Jr., tried in vain to plug the leaks in his Polish pup tent while Seattle-based flight attendant Kay Kolt talked Norwegian physician

Haakon "Hawk" Ragde into switching tents with her because a handsome Mongolian fishing guide named Bayara had just promised to "wisit her tonight." Wyoming construction mogul Park Gail and our perma-saturated tour leader, Tom Knight, chased off the lobotomizing effects of last night's Ghengis Khan Vodka with Chinese beer, and twenty-nine-year-old Oregon fly-fishing TV-show host Guido Rahr sat outside the lone cooking yurt tying flies. Stuart Burnett, a Hong Kong hotel executive, Granger Avery, a British Columbia country doctor, and Eric Peterson, co-owner of a fishing resort, were inside huddling around the cookstove beneath brightly painted ceiling spokes strung with several racks of rapidly aging mutton. The only audible voice was George Polatty's, who kept muttering: "Comm'nist bullshit."

Our fishing guides—Mongolians all—sat around their campfire some five yards from the yurt. Russian cigarettes fished for oxygen from the sides of their mouths as they sharpened the many hooks protruding from fishing lures made out of some sort of black Third World foam rubber—strange, porous obelisks meant to imitate a swimming Mongolian mouse. Once in a while, a hand would reach into a bag of little bakery cakes with indecipherable Mongolian symbols branded onto their tops, and every so often a cigarette ash would crash and burn on a knee and no one noticed.

This was the first day at fish camp. This was what we woke up to after a sleepless night spent between the one-inch Mongolian cotton mattresses that separated us from the ancient Mongolian earth, and the half-inch Mongolian horse blankets that weren't much help against the effects of subfreezing temperatures on flesh accustomed to central heating or, at least, goose down. This was Mongolia in June. Nothing to write home about, but then you'd get there three months before your letter would anyhow.

The night before had been better—real hotel beds in Ulan Bator, Outer Mongolia's bleak capital city. The train from Beijing had finally deposited us there after three days of Sino-Soviet weirdness, including a seven-hour Saturday night layover at the border, where we changed wheels to accommodate Mongolia's wider-gauge tracks. A few fishermen escaped to the border bar, where Russian soldiers threw back shots of Mongolian vodka while neon signs flashed in time to Eastern-bloc rock. The rest of us got locked in our sleeping car and sweated through that clanking, brutal surgery in the dark while "The Waltz of the Blue Danube" gargled out of the train station loudspeaker. From somewhere not far away, human screams ruptured the black spleen of the night. Then there was gunshot. "Ah don't know if they were shootin' at a rabbit or at us," George Polatty said, "but the screamin' sure stopped. Comm'nist bullshit."

As with other Soviet satellite countries at that time, the current Mongolian zeitgeist carried distinct anti-Russian sentiments as the country readied for its first free elections in seventy years. We had been warned to keep a low profile lest we be mistaken for

Russians and get the hell beaten out of us. Not exactly the most propitious time for a certain well-oiled American fishing guide to pump the many-medaled shoulder of a very large Mongolian customs officer and slur in no uncertain terms that we were "gonna catch the biggest f—in' fish in the world." Fortunately, the man refrained from reducing the offending fisherman to goat manure.

We spent the rest of the night crossing the Gobi Desert while its insidious grit stormed the failing shell of that old railroad mollusk, scouring our eyes and lungs raw, making miniature sand dunes against our windows and turning our hair to Brill-O. Sleep being a pipe dream, one found oneself falling into Fellini-esque conversations with, say, a Hungarian Professor named Dr. Lajosgooz who insisted that "Mongolians don't want to start agriculture because they don't want to hurt Mother Earth." Morning came on cool and bright, a mother-of-pearl sky edged in flat lace clouds. Antelope and wild camel loped across the taupe-colored earth for miles beyond our windows. "Looks just like Madison Basin in Montana," Frank Haw said. An attendant served us tea. In the dining car, the menu announced that "Food is Welcome" and we breakfasted on "Hot Animal Food," including "Borscht Moscow," steamed meat dumplings called "buuz," both kefir and "soured cream," and "fried eggs with fresh spring onions."

The air in Ulan Bator was charged and sharp. Built on the lap of the steppes, wild continental zephyrs play the capital's dreary collection of Soviet-designed blocks like dull chimes. The city feels huddled and lost, and urbanization remains an impossible command barked into the Mongolian wind.

The hotel air, like everything else, was laminated with mutton fat and the plumbing sounded like horns honking and donkeys braying. In the morning a maid walked right into my room and slammed the window shut, while a six-point bull elk trotted between the buses on the street below.

That time of year the winds bring the rains, and the great Mongolian plains bloom and soften . . . then turn to mud, the bottom-line of our all-day bus ride to fish camp—a chiropractor's horror movie, with very strange subtitles which Ed Brothers interpreted at regular intervals as "time to turn the other cheek." But our discomfort dissolved wholly at the feet of a vision burned once and forever into our burdened North American image banks: a lone herdsman. In a purple robe with a gold sash, a black bowler hat and tall black boots. Holding aloft a long, polished tree branch lance with a rope loop at its front end. Standing up in his stirrups and posting silently across Mongolia's extravagant grasslands.

Like the sites of all classic Western films, Mongolia is high plateau country. And our fish camp, when we finally got there, was slugged up in its northern forest on the green, green décolletage of a very pretty river valley. Birch and willow fluoresced chartreuse and new against the muddied ruin of the water. Our tents lay in the tender grasses above them. And the hills were alive with tamarack, not to mention wolves, wolverines, wild boar, Roe deer, elk, Siberian moose, pit vipers—which really prefer tender grasses—possibly snow leopard, and most certainly Asian brown bear, which were just waking up and thinking about going over the mountain to see what they could see.

On fishing trips, you can count on the natural beauty to nurture you when conditions can't. Or, as Kay Kolt put it: "I always give myself three days to catch a fish: one for weather, one to get to know the water and one for luck." My own fishing record is substantially less productive—about once a month I get lucky. The only explanation I've ever come up with is hormones: If I'm ovulating I'll catch every fish in the river. Unfortunately, this trip was going to miss my "O-Zone" by a week.

In barely mixed company, discussion topics naturally detour around any mention of feminine cycles. And with so many guy scientists in the group, questions tended to veer toward the academic, such as: How can a closed river system support such lunkers?

"Horses," Dr. Brothers replied, staring hopefully at the Mongolian minnows toodling around in his bucket.

We'd all seen the stories: "PEKING (UPI)—Thousands of Chinese tourists have visited a remote lake in western China to glimpse a horse-eating water monster. . . ." And, "At least 50 horses and a dozen men have been eaten alive by a 35-foot fish that swallows its victims whole, the New China News Agency reports." These clips, supplied, it turned out, by Brothers himself, were part of the Mongolia hype distributed to all us eager anglers.

For twenty years, the agency has taken big-game hunters into this boreal wilderness in pursuit of Mongolia's macro-rack elk. With the civilized world finally waking up to the deep creepiness of trophy hunting, the agency decided to add fishing to its repertoire. When I heard about this once-in-a-lifetime chance to be part of the First Western Mongolian Salmon Fishing Expedition, I suffered a serious glee attack. Salmon are my totem. My original call of the wild. They are role models for three of the traits I value most: tenacity, courage and passion. I even met my husband in an Alaskan salmon smokery—our wedding rings are twin gold salmon joined at the tail. The only way I'd be kept from fishing Mongolia in person was if they built a dam between my house and the airport.

When I finally arrived I was hypnotized. Mongolia is ravishing, like the Great Plains before contact, an endless wind-washed grassland slung between forested edges and mountains so old and wind-worn you felt like scampering up one just to get a God's-eye view of the place.

"Damn if it doesn't look like western Montana," Frank Haw said again, nodding at the handsome woodlands around us.

"Montana with cuckoo clocks," Brothers grumbled.

Nine times in the last seven minutes, we had been obliged to suffer what Austrians must endure only once an hour—the demented call of the cuckoo, which surely would be Mongolia's state bird, if the place were a state.

Mongolia was then, in fact, a Communist republic—the Mongolian People's Republic—and had been since 1924. It's big . . . and empty—about four times the size of Montana, slightly larger than Alaska, with the population of Oregon. Actually, most Mongols have migrated to Chinese territory, having been run off by the Communists, the cuckoo birds, the weather (minus fifty-four degrees one winter), and names that look like the bottom line of an eye-chart. Agbaanjantsangiyn Jamsranjab, for instance, Mongolia's then Minister of Public Security, and Choyjiljabyn Tserennadmid, its then Minister of Health, and its former president, Punsalmaagiin Ochirbat. You can see the allure of a hundred million Wongs.

The Mongols who stayed home are super-Mongolians. Bored silly with Soviet dweebiness, they had, not long before our visit, called for a cultural renaissance, bringing back Ghengis Khan, the Mongolian alphabet and the golden *soyombo*—the Mongolian national emblem consisting of a flame, the sun, the moon, two triangles, four rectangles and, Mongolian Mystery #2: two FISH! All of which explains why our interpreter, mercifully named Basa, looked like a Nepalese rabbi. Like the lone herdsman, he walked around camp in a brown robe sashed with gold—the traditional Mongolian dress code, give or take color choice.

Mongolia is still ninety percent grasslands, and half of its 2.1 million people are still nomadic, running their twenty-five million horses, goats, camels and sheep over the wide open steppes. They have Aleut good looks—brown skin, Asian eyes, cheekbones like hard-boiled eggs—and a rumored national proclivity for promiscuity that has earned Mongolia the nickname "Sweden of the south."

This fact titillated our boys enough to instantly inspire a trip motto: "Swe-den! Swe-den!" . . . until our own Dr. Ragde, a prostate specialist, broke the news that Mongolia hosts a virtual smorgasbord of venereal diseases, many of which are untreatable and lethal. Thus did our fisherman's war cry revert to the original: "Cuckoo. Cuckoo."

The second morning flowered above us like the wild iris that bloom all over northern Outer Mongolia in June. The sky looked like Liz Taylor's eyes, and the river looked like the rest of her. Though still out of shape, its big belly had gone down an inch or so, and fishing parties were organized. That day I fished with Polatty, Peterson, Rahr, Burnett and Avery.

After a breakfast of bread, butter, Rumanian cherry jam, instant coffee glazed with a film of mutton fat and cubed Mongolian mutton, and after Hawk Ragde led a successful campaign to trade six bottles of vodka and two cases of beer for at least one sleeping yurt, we headed out. We had been promised sleeping yurts with wood floors. We had also been promised a "Soviet-built four-wheel-drive vehicle with driver and an English-speaking interpreter for each two clients." What we had was Pup Tents from Hell, a jeep, a flat-bed truck . . . and Basa. And an assortment of local guides who could only say "Elvees Presleey," except for Bayara, that Mongolian Romeo, who clearly picked up his English from Prince albums. We all piled into the truck and took off downriver.

Being a girl in a seriously macho country has its advantages— I got to sit in the cabin with the driver, Tim-ul, and look at the "Welcome to Mongolia" stickers on the dash. Each one featured a different animal: elk, deer, bighorn sheep, snow leopard, moose, a drooling brown bear. Tim-ul pointed to the wolf sticker and made a gunning engine noise: "Chun! Chun!" Then he did a git-along-little-doggies motion with his hands and said, "Yo-*ho!* Yo-*ho!,*" Mongolian for "go," burying the "o" sound like those pit-of-the-stomach German words that mean "he has hair on his teeth." Mostly, though, Mongolian sounds like a kind of ancient gut music spoken by a people who have the wind of the steppes in their souls.

Our group was let off last. We did not get Basa. We got "Fish Master," whose real name sounded like "Tigshee," which certain incorrigible members of the group secretly mistook for a certain barnyard by-product.

Fish Master had made it clear to Basa that we Westerners had already made three critical mistakes: "too much luggage, too thin fishing line and too small hooks." Mongolians fish to catch fish. They do not understand the sport of trying to take a big one on the lightest line possible. They think that's cuckoo.

Fish Master also regarded our super flies with disgust. Given taimen's carnivorous reputation, we had been busy tying huge Mariboo Muddlers with spun deer-hair heads, white and black mariboo wings, and silver-and-gold tinseled bodies. Gaudy, nine-inch Las Vegas monsters that would give any American trout heart failure. We were also well stocked with giant deer-hair mice called Lefty's Deceivers. And Guido had tied some sinewy macro-streamers with colored synthetic hair that looked like Magic Pony roadkill.

Given our sorry lure selection, Fish Master felt it necessary to demonstrate the overriding wisdom of the Swimming Mongolian Mouse. Having led us swiftly across difficult terrain riffled with dirt mounds to which he pointed and made wild boar snorts, we finally broke through a stand of birch and found ourselves on an elbow of sandy beach. In a stunning breach of American fishing-guide etiquette, Fish Master cast first. Upstream, no less. He drew his floating mouse across the old Hongoi River and got nothing. He cast again and got a substantial strike. "Tuul," he said coolly, which is Mongolian for taimen, and reeled in with strange, subtle jerks. The fish surfaced sluggishly, flashing salmon-colored fins. It had no fight in it and an ugly green triangular head. Fish Master beached it proudly. It weighed fourteen pounds.

Fish Master then decided to examine my tackle, which, at the moment, was one of the smart little deer-hair mice Guido had tied out of caribou fur lifted from an old rug in the cooking yurt. He had set up a vise right there, tied on a little leather mousey tail, then held the caribou in small bundles and spun it around the shank of the hook until the ends flared out. He packed it up the head of the hook, tied on two little leather ears, then spun more caribou hair behind the hook's eye to make a little varmint head. Finally he gave the thing a haircut, shaping it lovingly into a damn respectable facsimile of a mouse.

Fish Master pronounced it useless, gave it the equivalent of a Mongolian raspberry and looted Polatty's tackle box until he found a simple brass French lure called a Mepps #5. He tied it to my line with the exasperated motions of a parent wiping chocolate off the face of a child in church. Against my deepest philosophical values I tried the thing and instantly got a small taimen, which my conscience bade me lose in the shallows.

When Fish Master stopped pestering me, I secretly switched back to my little rug-rat fly and cast fruitlessly but happily away into the Montana light of a Mongolian afternoon.

All in all, our group took a couple of graylings and a good-sized lenok, which is an unremarkable fish except for being the oldest species of trout in the world, and that was about it for the rest of the day.

The new sleeping yurt was up by the time we got back to camp. Polatty, Brothers, Avery, Burnett, Ragde and Kolt abandoned their pup tents for a space on its tender grassy floor. We were further heartened by the announcement that dinner duties that night would be taken over by Eric Peterson, who had responded to pretrip warnings of Mongolia's subgustatory cuisine by lugging in two jumbo coolers stocked with Dijon, marmalade, wasabe, gherkins, whole pepper corns and a grinder, rosemary, thyme, oregano, curry powder, Korean kimchee, Swiss soup mix, Japanese ramen, an arsenal of English biscuits, Italian olive oil, French pâté, Norwegian sardines, smoked oysters, anchovy paste, Jarlsberg cheese, American peanut butter, a case of fine wine, fresh produce from Beijing and many jars of Russian caviar plucked from Ulan Bator's black market. Chinese and Mongolian customs officers naturally assumed he was neck-deep in some international gourmet import scam with Ed Brothers.

Peterson opted to cook up Fish Master's taimen which Brothers offered to fillet. He was really after its otoliths, tiny, leaf-shaped ear stones lodged deep in a fish's head. Brothers is one of the world's experts at aging fish by reading their ear stones, but first he has to suck the gunk off them with his mouth. While people held their stomachs and pretended to look at the scenery, Slime-Breath Brothers finally announced that Fish Master's taimen was around ten years old. Its flesh was firm and creamy white and looked—and, once cooked, tasted—a lot like trout. While the welcomed perfumes of Chinese garlic and lemon rode the air around the cooking yurt, Dr. Brothers also reported that his net had taken yet another species.

"The family common name is loach," he said, displaying an uneventful-looking fish. Then he told us that a tropical cousin of the one he caught gets hyperactive when low pressure fronts move in, and is, therefore, called the "weather fish."

"There's also an air-breathing loach whose gut tissue stores oxygen," Brothers added. "When the barometric pressure changes, it flips over and flatulates out its air. We call those the 'farting weather fish.'" As people backed away from Brothers and his fish bucket, Fish Master told Basa to tell us that we would go fishing that night.

"After dinner?" Dr. Ragde asked, imagining a good evening bite.

"No, at midnight," Basa translated.

Cuckoo. Cuckoo.

Fishing on a moonless midnight in Outer Mongolia with non-English-speaking guides who had Ghengis Khan Vodka for supper takes guts. More than I had, but then I'd learned that equation in high school: Boys + Alcohol + Fast Cars = Health Hazard 101. Nonetheless, Eric Peterson went. So did Polatty, Avery, Burnett, Rahr and Brothers, who fishes for brown trout late June nights in the upper Delaware River back home in Ithaca and somehow missed the Alcohol + Fast Cars part. He had even tied his own version of the Swimming Mongolian Mouse for the event—a trimmed-spun-elk-hair rodent with a chamois tail, which he christened the "Lemming Meringue Fly."

They took the jeep and the truck, the drivers of which played chicken in the dark the whole way. And in case a bear showed up, the fishing guides also took guns, one of which was on the floor of the truck cabin pointed at Eric Peterson's head.

Guido didn't like the idea of night fishing with guns. "It's too dark to see anything," he said. "If you hit a bear, you'd probably just wound it."

Rahr, Basa and one of the drivers hiked over to a wide, deep pool in the Sharlon River, a tributary, like the Hongoi, of the Uro River, which began at their confluence just downstream from our fish camp. Stars glittered through the treetops like animal eyes, and the river looked like it was filled with eels. Rahr waded up to his waist and cast into the darkness, trying not to remember the UPI stories about horse-eating fish. "If the big ones do come out at night," he thought, "I'm hamburger."

Suddenly, there was a commotion upstream. The driver had just lost a fish on single forty-pound test line. He had been fishing with a double strand forty-pound test leader, and he had been fishing a Mongolian mouse the size of a rat with three sets of hooks. The fish broke off two inches above the lure. Both strands of the leader were badly frayed. The fish had swallowed the mouse whole.

So the *Hucho* honchos *were* there. And even though in seventeen years of fishing Fish Master's best catch was only an eighty-pound taimen, Rahr shifted into high gear. He dead-drifted the riffles. He worked the pools. He dragged the tailouts. Fishing blind, he cast and cast again into the black Mongolian night. He didn't catch a thing. But he couldn't help hoping there was a big one out there somewhere, waiting for Guido.

George Polatty came closer the following day, our third day at fish camp and second day of fishing. Avoiding yet another bread and mutton breakfast, he and Park Gail left camp early to fish the Sharlon. After catching one too many lenok, Polatty switched to a Mepps #5 spinner and got a serious strike. It was a taimen. It jumped clean out of the water three times, dove straight down and jumped again. It didn't run. They never do. Finally it rolled over on the line and broke off. Polatty says it was six feet long and weighed a good eighty pounds. Gail agrees.

Meanwhile, Guido and I had about drowned our deer-hair mice and showgirl streamer patterns. And we had precious little to show for it. By dinnertime, none of us had landed the kind of newsmaker jumbo salmon we had come for. All we had was a mess of little lenok and grayling. Morale was knee-high to a pit viper, and we were all ready to request cuckoo bird hors d'oeuvres. Instead we were treated to a local specialty—smoked lenok, which our fishing guides prepared whole over their campfire. It was fabulous, a miracle of smoky tenderness, and it swiftly generated Mongolian Mystery #3: Just how does a populace that doesn't fish know how to make bar mitzvah-quality lox?

Around noon the next day a Soviet helicopter landed in the field in front of our camp. A clutch of Mongolians in 1957 Western clothes deplaned and walked toward the cooking yurt. Basa addressed them, then explained they were from the Ministry of the Protection of Nature. Delighted—and relieved—we requested an audience. After some twenty minutes, we were invited inside. The men were seated cross-legged on the floor or lounging around on the rugs, Mongolian style, sipping tea. I asked about the future of Western fishing expeditions there. Their leader, a Mr. Badam, said, "Western fishermen are welcome," and he "wishes us success." Then we were dismissed. The officials stayed in the cooking yurt for several hours. They had come, it was clear, for lunch. George Polatty shook his head, "Comm'nist bullshit."

By midafternoon it was seventy-five degrees and the river looked very good. Guido Rahr and I walked upstream to the

Mother of All Bridges and cast a few under it, still overworking our deer mice to the point of exhaustion. Guido was more frustrated than I was. Maybe it was the wrong time of the month, but my killer instinct had curled up in the sun with a good book. Mongolia or no, the place felt like home, abloom with all the appointments that make fishing rivers so grand—the dry flutter of tree leaves, the blue eye of the sky, a soothing breeze, real air, the Champagne chill of the water and its uncorked musical gargle.

Many anglers confess to the fact that before long they expect to be happy just standing around in nature with nothing much to do, that catching a fish even now is secondary to fishing and may become utterly unnecessary. I, myself, was hovering on the cusp of such passive angling contentment when Brothers walked by. He'd been fishing the Sharlon and told us about a new pool he'd found. "I was trailing an ugly rabbit-hair Dahlberg Diver there," he reported, "and on my second cast this huge green head came up behind the fly—must have been a good six or seven inches between the eyes. It opened its mouth, then just closed it again and slowly sank back down." And that was it for the Pacifist Within. Without a word Guido and I packed up and headed for Ed's Pool.

We hiked upriver through iris and yellow poppies and banks of what looked to be wild strawberry heavy with white blossoms. The *soyombo* sun blazed above, turning the river to chrome, and you couldn't help wondering why Mongolia didn't look less like the foothills of the American Rockies and more like Pluto.

Ed's Pool was a beautiful thing. Quiet, like jade slag trimmed in a cowl of sandy beach. Granite cliffs rose heavenward on the other side, crowned with stands of birch. It was as if we were fishing a subterranean stream in the basement of the forest, and the strangesse it produced somehow made us come to our senses. Our big deer-hair flies just weren't working. It was time for a change.

"Let's fish for these guys the way we know how," Guido suggested while I was already digging around for some little black nymphs, wet flies that imitate deep-water insect larvae.

We should have thought of this before. Even Ed had reported that the fish in this pool took one look at his big gawd-awful frog patterns and just turned around.

I cast into the long run below the pool and let my fly swing at the end of the drift. Bam! A lenok hit within seconds. It fought like a somewhat freaked-out champ, albeit one shocked by what surely must have been its first time to be hoisted through the water by its lip. When I released it the poor thing almost spontaneously combusted with relief.

Guido got one next, and then another; I landed a fourth. Then Guido remembered that he had some lead-eyed sculpin in his fly box left over from a fishing trip to the Yellow Breeches River near Harrisburg, Pennsylvania. They had black mariboo tails, black chenille bodies and black deer-hair heads studded with little black sticking-out lead eyes that made them sink, a classic fly pattern developed for the region's brown trout. Limestone Stream Brownies, they call them, native to the Yellow Breeches as well as Spring Creek and Pennsylvania Creek—famous trout streams all, where some of the first American fly-fishing began more than a hundred years ago. Old sculpin patterns like those seemed an appropriate offering to the ancient waters of Mongolia where they would surely imitate one of Ed Brothers's little black loaches swimming hard.

Guido cast first. Instantly, a fish hit—a big lenok. He released it and cast again. His cream-colored line drew pale snakes in the air. "I feel lucky," he said, an angler's magic words. His announcement activated my finest fishing manners. I stayed off the water.

Guido's lead-eyed sculpin sailed into the deepest corner of the pool, and like the counterweight of a theater drape, when it sank, the curtain rose. From somewhere offstage, the Mongolian Weather Gods blew a sudden strong wind upriver, and the birch leaves rattled overhead like money. Rolling thunder exploded in the aisle of sky above us and the songbirds went nuts, shrieking alarms and dive-bombing my hair. The air smelled possessed, full of ozone and ions, and the clouds kept doubling over and then standing up taller than before. Finally, like a play within a play, Guido Rahr got a major fish on.

"This is it," he said. "I'm going for a world record."

In a swirl of peach tail fin, the fish turned and Guido turned with it, his right arm flung out sideways like Nureyev. The fish took a dive, and Guido let it run, his reel spinning in the palm of his hand. The taimen turned again, and again Guido stepped gracefully aside, locked into the holy communion between fisherman and fish, the water ballet that renders angling angelic, elevating the sport beyond the usual life and death struggle. When the rain came twenty minutes later, Guido beached his fish, an eleven-pound beautiful-ugly Mongolian *Hucho hucho* taimen, the king of the wild frontier.

Then it was my turn. I cast far, letting the heavy eyes of the sculpin sink to the sandy bottom and drift left. The rain-stippled surface of the river blurred my water vision, and I tried to use my fly like physical sonar, letting it bounce the contours of the river bottom back across my index finger in hopeful jolts and hops.

Guido saw it first, surfacing in an ungodly display of triangular terribleness. Flat green head, sick orange skin, Ed's Monster Taimen. It was, there is no doubt, my one and only chance to land the world's biggest—and ugliest—salmon on a fly; however, my instincts had other ideas. Let's just say that my body reacted to that rising mass of icky ichthyology the same way it did when my computer screen filled with pulsing green "V's" and announced "Internal Stack Failure. Exit Now!" And I ran screaming out of the room . . . or, in this case, the river. I'd be damned if I was going to set a world record with a fish that looked so much like Quasimodo in a mermaid suit that I was afraid to be in the water with it.

The storm delivered many Mongolian salmon that day. Granger Avery took a fourteen-pounder as long as his arm. So did Frank Haw, on eight-pound test. George Polatty landed a five-pound taimen on four-pound test. "I reckon I got a world record with this one," he reckoned. He reckoned right. No one from the West had ever fished taimen before; the International Game Fish Association had no categories for them. You could catch a quarter-pound taimen with a stick and set a world record. We were competing only against ourselves.

Kay Kolt was right. It had taken three days to nail these bozos, lightweights that they were. This conditional victory is the only explanation for the ensuing Night of Mongolian Madness. After supper, everyone just piled into the sleeping yurt and pounded down several bottles of Genghis Khan. At 3:00 a.m., the yurt still glowed like a fallen star beneath the Mongolian night, and if you listened closely, between the animal cries and the call of the cuckoo you could make out the party's theme song:

"Tai-ai-ai-men is on my line, yes it is!"

By noon the next day ninety percent of the anglers were still sleeping it off. With the noble exception of Ed Brothers, who, despite a ripping case of vodka fog, went fishing and finally got his record-setting taimen, a ten-pounder on eight-pound test. He would have used four, but that's what Rahr had taken his fish on, so Brothers switched to eight to ensure world records for both of them.

We would submit four: Polatty's and Haw's in the Freshwater Line classes, Brothers's and Rahr's in the Fly Rod catagory. And, in the end, Haw's eight-pound line would test out at twelve, Polatty's four-pound line would test out at eight, and so would Rahr's, knocking Brothers's slightly lighter fish caught on certified eight-pound line out of the world record book forever.

Our last day at fish camp broke like a raw egg, the yolk of the sun sliding down the backside of a very misty morning. Everyone was busy packing when Ed Brothers and George Polatty discovered the pit viper between their bedrolls. It was a young one, but it definitely had a pit, a heat-seeking hole beside one nostril, which explains what it was doing in the sleeping yurt.

Polatty had picked it up to examine it, holding it behind its head, when one of the Mongolians came racing down the river bank screaming "Bear!" It was definitely time to go home.

In a suite at the Hotel Ulan Bator that night, a special meeting was held. Frank Haw, Ed Brothers, Guido Rahr, Tom Knight and I wanted a chance to discuss Mongolian fish conservation with

Basa and his boss, Mr. Bator, the president of Zhuulchin, Mongolia's official travel agency, which arranges all trips.

We knew Mongolia was ripe for the late twentieth century, full of copper, gold, silver, coal and, unfortunately, oil, which both American and British industrialists can't wait to get their hands on. We knew that Japan had already entered into a joint venture with Mongolia to manufacture steel, cashmere and electronics, and JAL Airlines was trying to establish a direct route from Tokyo to Ulan Bator. We knew Mongolia was moving fast toward economic development. But we hoped that in this initial rush to be like the West, we Westerners might offer a word of caution, an educated plea that Mongolians value what Mongolia is and has managed to remain, while the rest of the world plunders itself into a toxic coma.

"Taimen are *precious*," I practically pleaded.

"They really are rare," Brothers confirmed.

"We'll send you a book on the biology of these fish," Haw offered.

"Dis book *wery* useful," Basa replied. "Vee *need* information."

"In my reading I've learned that these fish are getting more and more scarce," Haw went on. "There's no reason not to practice catch-and-release."

"You don't have to kill a fish," our suddenly animated, ever-besotted leader Tom Knight offered. "You can make a fiberglass replica of it."

"You should know that a number of streams in the United States are catch-and-release only," I said.

"We have catch-and-release streams *and* kill streams," Rahr reminded. "And it's not fair to lock off streams from the locals."

"All along the rivers we saw evidence of local fishing," Knight said.

"Mongolians, they don't listen," Basa replied. "We do have licenses."

"There are legal problems," Mr. Bator admitted. "Inspectors come maybe four times a month."

"You need to develop a plan," Haw said.

"We've found that local nonprofit organizations can be an enormous help," Rahr said.

"Yes," I concurred, sending small conspiratorial eye-daggers to Guido. "They do the work our government *should* be doing."

"Vee might start a fish association party," Basa replied. "I have dis in my head to do."

"How can we call it?" Mr. Bator asked. "The National Foundation of Fish?"

Tom Knight grinned. "Hey, we're in on the ground floor of a fisheries management program, here!"

"You'll want to be careful about damming, too," Haw went on.

"Dams stop migration and can wipe out a whole run of fish," Rahr warned.

"Oh, our Green Party is fighting against dis," Basa informed us. "Dey want zero dams planned for beeg rivers."

"THE GREEN PARTY?" Everyone gasped. "In *Mongolia?*"

"Oh, yes," Basa replied. "Vee have dee Green Party and many nature parties. But vee don't have a fish party." He paused for a moment, and then he smiled. "Mongolian fishes are wery lucky, maybe," he said. "Vee are a Buddhist country, and Buddhism says, 'Don't touch snakes and vater animals.' Until I vas fifteen years old, I vas told by my mother, 'Don't touch fishes—dis is evil to do.' Dis is maybe a good ting."

And this maybe meant that Mongolia was in better shape than we thought it was. Maybe, then, we could all go home knowing we could come back in ten years and the Big Green Ones would still be out there with the snow leopards and the bears, the wolves and the wild boar and the idiotic cuckoos, despite the fact that Brothers had lobbied hard for year-round open season on them. And maybe in ten years we'd still have to take a bone-busting bus ride to fish camp, and somewhere along the way our hearts would thrill again to the sight of a lone Mongolian cowboy, dressed like Ghengis Khan himself, riding high in his saddle across the generous purple steppes of Outer Mongolia.

La Serenissima: Italy

If the Italian Renaissance painters had been dentists, their dentures would have looked like Venice. Arcaded and cupolaed, welded together with fancy bridgework, riddled with elegant root canals, its yellowed buildings rising straight out of the sea, it looks, for all the world, like a floating grin.

In truth, Venice has every reason to be grinning. No city on earth went so far, did so much, with so little. There are no forests. There are no farms. No veins of gold ever marbled the mud of its oozing foundation. There are no hills from which to quarry anything worth sculpting. And God only knows where it gets its drinking water.

However.

What Venice did have was position, and the brains to use it. For a thousand years it sat on the cusp of Europe and Asia, straddling East and West, and quietly fleeced both sides. They called Venice "La Serenissima," the Serene One.

The city traded in exotica, in emeralds and spice, ebony and silk, in parrots, ivory and pearls. All the scented tinsel of the Orient funneled through its busy port en route to the courts of England and France, and Venice became ridiculously wealthy.

The riches began to slip away in 1453 when the Muslims took Constantinople, with whom Venice had a historically lucrative, if questionable, trade agreement. Then, in 1498, Vasco da Gama opened a new trade route to India by sailing around the Cape of Good Hope, and the Venetian monopoly ended forever.

Napoleon finished Venice off 300 years later, claiming the republic as his own, saying, "Dust to ashes, dead and done with, Venice spent what Venice earned."

Well, not exactly.

Some things never change, and Venice is one of them. Yes, its wealth has mostly dribbled away to Rome and Milan. There are only eight of the original ruling families' names left in the phone book, and there's no one home at the doge's palace anymore. But that old Venetian spirit is still going strong. Tourism is the business of the day, and it is no accident that Venetians are making a handsome living from charging people to come see the city that they built by charging people.

"That's 45,000 lira," Amando told me as I stepped into his glossy black gondola. I scrambled for my calculator.

"That's thirty dollars!" I gasped.

Amando shrugged. "It's a long way," he said. "And it's dangerous. I have to take you into the lagoon. Could break my boat."

I was changing hotels, and there are two ways to move things in Venice: by boat or by back—your back or, more precisely, your hands, if you're lugging luggage—and guidebooks are filled with warnings of the tenacity of the Venetian blister (it seems to have something to do with the damp weather and trudging up and down all those little bridges). So I agreed. Like Europe in the Middle Ages, I had no choice.

But Venetians are charming pirates. While taking you with one hand, they will entertain you lavishly with the other, and Amando was no exception. He looked like Fred MacMurray. He acted like Zorba the Greek. He wore a white straw hat with a red ribbon that streamed down his back. And he sang "O so-low mi-o" for the tourists, who clicked their cameras down at us from little white bridges.

"Ho!" Amando yelled up to them. "Is anybody coming?"

He could see perfectly well that nobody was coming.

"We have to go the long way," he said. "The sea's too rough today."

The short way would have been to head straight for the lagoon, turn left and glide half a mile north to my new hotel. The long way meant threading through the watery filigree of Venice's back canals—back alleys in any other city. But here they are capillaries, a twisting matrix of transport, a gelatinous medium of connection binding the city's 118 mini-islands into one. As Amando performed his splendid pilotry, slipping us neatly under bridges with a single push of his single pole, missing other boats by the quarter inch, you couldn't help but wonder how a place as strange as this could ever come to be.

From the air Venice looks like a swordfish or two wrenches fighting or Pacman biting the gloved hand of an important magistrate, depending on your century. It is divided down the center by a snaking land-gap called the Grand Canal and is crissed and crossed and packed and parceled into a solid-state brick and marble mosaic by smaller canalworks.

The city is about a mile and a half across at its widest and three and a half miles long. It sits in 200 square miles of saltwater in the northwestern crescent of the Adriatic, protected from the open sea by long sandy ribbons of littoral. If Italy wears a boot, then the Venetian lagoon is a blue mole on the back of its upper thigh.

The lagoon is a quiet place, like a saline lake, and it is the natural dump for the half dozen rivers that feed it, crashing down from the high Italian Alps and fanning into the Venetian estuaries, bringing their sediment and grit with them. Century after century, the sediment built up, in shoals and mud flats, in marshes and bogs—a most enriched environment if you're a clam or a mosquito, but not exactly paradise for the rest of us. In fact, the rest of us would have just as soon stayed home on the mainland. But Attila the Hun had other ideas. So did the Goths and Vandals and other battle-ax barbarians who swooped down on Italy without permits in the fifth and sixth centuries. So rough were their invasions, so nasty their intentions, that the local citizens eventually just got out of their way, taking refuge in the soggy peace and safety of the Venetian islands. And so, like it or not, they became pioneers. They built new churches, devised new institutions and developed new governments. They also fought bitterly among themselves over the details for centuries, until they finally decided that since they were in this mess together, they might as well act like it. And in 687 A.D., they elected a president, called a doge (pronounced "dough-jay"), the first of an unbroken line of 117 such creatures, each reigning for life as the gilt and glitter symbol of a thousand years of merciless mercantile madness.

Which is ultimately why I found myself sitting in this ruinously expensive shoe of a boat with its silly metal figurehead—"like the doge's hat"—thumping along on the choppy waves of the lagoon while Amando struggled to deliver me to my front door, which was, much to my delight, right on the water.

I had done what most tourists do when they arrive in Venice after dark sans reservations: take the first available vacancy. I got a dungeon of a room with no heat, no bathroom and a chorus of drunk Germans stationed beneath my window.

So, early the next morning I started walking. I wanted sun and silence at the right price, the combination of which set my breakfast waiter's tongue to clicking.

"Non poss-ee-blay," he said.

Still I walked. Past the Piazza San Marco, the dubious heart of tourist territory with its permanent supply of pigeons and pigeon by-products. Past the lavish lagoon hotels, their Byzantine windows flaring with the dawn. Past the docked water buses still lashed together for overnight security and slamming into each other with alarming force at every passing wave. Past the armies of mainland workmen emptying out of the first ferries with their lunches under their arms and their collars turned up against the chill. Past the bakeries, their yeast and sugar perfumes rising toward the hissing kiss of adjoining espresso bars.

Nuns I passed, even monks, and many purposeful Venetian dogs, their noses locked into metal muzzles. Bridges I climbed, while boats heavy with apples and cabbages from the Po Valley slid beneath me and disappeared down one of Venice's many throats on their way to restaurants deep in the municipal midsection.

To my right a tanker inched by, while the high heels of a Venetian matron snippity-snapped on the ancient stones of the city's sidewalks, then faded in the opposite direction. And suddenly I began to feel a new freedom, an energy I'd never felt before in an American city. It was a fuel-injected synchromesh shock-absorbing cruise-controlled high-performance human sense of ease. And it came from one glorious fact: *There are no cars in Venice*.

The motorized mess of the late twentieth century is not Venice's legacy: Venice belongs to people. And few other Western cities are better at making you feel like you're still part of the tribe.

The Bucintoro, namesake of the doge's own golden barge and the hotel of my dreams, sat pink and shimmering in that vaporous Venetian light. Yes, they had a vacancy, yes, with a bathroom, yes, many windows, yes, on the top floor, yes, yes, on the water, yes, breakfast included, yes, available now. Yes, I took it. And it became my private, sun-flooded, tourist-proof retreat in a city that provides all other creature comforts as a matter of course.

That settled, it was time for my next priority: food. It's no use trying to give directions to my numerous Venetian culinary discoveries—I don't know where they are. That's because the best way to find a great meal in Venice is the best way to find anything in Venice: Get lost. Guidebooks only lead you to other tourists reading the same guidebooks. I tried following people who looked particularly Venetian—tailored, self-possessed, scented and pale—but they kept disappearing into banks. The only thing left to do was surrender to the walking rhythm of the city, enjoy the opportunity to not get run over by a Toyota, welcome the mind-curdling network of dark and narrow passageways, and try not to fall into a canal.

That's what I did and that's how I found tiny bistros serving exquisite local squid cooked in its own ink and great yellow slabs of Venetian polenta; bakeries featuring just-baked Torta Venezia, fragrant with raisins and anise; cafes whose cappuccino was as frothy as whipped cream; Harry's Bar, whose bean soup did not warrant Hemingway's generous recommendation; endless shops filled with fleece-lined pale gray suede boots, Valentino originals at unaffordable prices, coral beads "from Napoli," lace tablecloths "from Burano," tacky glass seabirds "from Murano;" and the open market at Rialto Bridge, its fruits and vegetables enriched by the alpine topsoil of nearby farms.

It is also how I found Nonna, Rufina and the San Marco Trattoria.

They were sisters. Exiled daughters of czarist Russia. They were remarkably beautiful, with their black dresses and white hair, and they happened to be sitting at the table next to mine.

"We came here by chance," Nonna explained. "And we have been coming here ever since and it hasn't changed a bit in twenty years. You know, there are the places that are supposed to be the top, the expensive places, and over the years they have all deteriorated. Everything now is so mass-produced."

"My darling, it is, in one word, revolting," Rufina agreed. "But, you see, here they don't cook big quantities. It's fresh. And it is like eating in the best of homes. Here, you must try their torta. She made it," she said, waving to the woman in the kitchen. Then Rufina called the waitress by name and ordered me a slice of cream and chocolate sin.

"Are you Italian or English?" I asked.

"Well," Rufina replied, "we're neither. We're Russian. White Russian. Our parents left in 1922 when we were small children and the rest of our family was murdered. We live in London now, and we have no one left but our elder sister, who lives in a convent there."

"Ah, there's nowhere like Venice in the world," Nonna added. "It still knows how to live."

I asked if I could take their picture. Rufina instructed me to take her sister's picture.

"I am absolutely old," she said, and then asked, "What have you photographed? Surely you have seen the cathedral. Have you been back behind the altar and seen the Pala d'Oro?"

I shook my head, somewhat embarrassed at having given Venice's priceless treasures a back seat to my search for the perfect hotel.

"You haven't seen it?" she said, her voice rising at the end like an incredulous schoolteacher. She turned and spoke to her sister in rapid Russian, threw her napkin down on the table, stood up and said, "We take you there now."

~

Adjacent to the stone lace of the doge's palace, on the north side of the Piazza San Marco, sits the Basilica, the most famous church in Venice. It used to be the doge's private chapel. Now it's gone public and it will—for a small fee—swallow you down into its several magnificent bellies.

Rufina insisted on paying. Nonna had insisted on staying behind, knowing there was nothing she could add to her sister's gift of instruction when it came to art, especially religious art.

Rufina tied a scarf on her head, knelt and crossed herself several times in front of the cathedral's great door, then she kissed her hand.

"We are Orthodox, Russian Orthodox," she said in a hushed voice. "And this is how we do it. Now, come. And mind your step, it is a stone sea."

I looked down, startled by the warped marble mosaics that rolled across the old church floor.

"The bones of Saint Mark are over there," Rufina whispered, waving toward the back of the cathedral. "He was evangelizing Alexandria—it was a great center of Christianity in those days—and he died there in eight hundred and something. I forget now, but there was a Saracen prince who wanted to enlarge his palace, and the church where Saint Mark's relics were in Alexandria was going to be destroyed. The Christian priest and the monk were very upset about this, and they met two merchants from Venice and as the Muslim people don't eat pork, they gave the body of Saint Mark to the merchants in a huge basket covered with hams so that the Muslims wouldn't look at what was carried. That's how he came to Venice. He is now the patron saint of Venice. Wherever you go, you see the lion because it is the symbol of the gospel of Saint Mark.

"Now. You must see the Pala d'Oro. It is one of the finest treasures in Venice."

The huge rectangular panel stood behind an altar at the far end of the cathedral. Its front was ablaze with rubies and emeralds, sapphires and pearls, topazes, amethysts and cloisonné figures, all set in blinding gold. Rufina took a moment to drink in its luminosity, then she began.

"Look. Here you have Christ and the angels, you have Our Lady, you have saints, you have prophets, you have everything, and on the side you even have the story of Saint Mark being brought here. Beautiful."

As we left, we passed the ornate tomb of Saint Mark, and Rufina quickly kissed its white linen hem and crossed herself again. Then she led me to the treasury, which was a museum really, full of brilliant Byzantine chalices, alabaster altar ornaments, carved agate figurines, mother-of-pearl communion trays and bejeweled crucifixes. Rufina moved gracefully among them, noting details, telling stories, seeing something special and holy in each one. Perhaps it was just a quirk of light, but in her presence they seemed to glow with a force far grander than the precious skin of their own aristocratic beauty. It must have had something to do with faith, with the private essences we bring to things, because it didn't seem to bother Rufina in the slightest that these glittery artifacts—in fact, most of the opulent flourishes of this church—were the booty of the Fourth Crusade, ripped from Constantinople by the crews of Doge Enrico Dandolo in what historians call the greatest crime in history.

On our way out of the Basilica, Rufina stopped to light an amber candle from her elder sister's convent and placed it on the small public altar. Once outside, we said good-bye, and as Rufina turned to leave, a silver hair pin slid from her hair and tumbled to the ground. I stooped to pick it up for her, but by then she had disappeared into the circus of tourists and birds, now bleached and blurred in the dazzling light of a Venetian afternoon.

The Wild Life

Day of the Stiff Dogs

Call me a retro-nerd. Call me a gonzo naturalist. But when it comes to being impressed by genius, the Wild Kingdom wins over the Silicon Valley every time. Would computer wizard Steve Wozniak keep his teeth in his stomach, and his stomach in his head? Or replace a lost eye with a nose? The Maine lobster does. If a large gator attacked microchip genie Bill Gates, could Gates cast off his leg, then grow back another? The starfish can. This alone is reason enough for technobrats to remember to take a field trip every once in a while.

And it's a good excuse to launch a great American bio-quest, searching for bizarre bugs and animals whose daily habits make MTV look like a Mormon Tabernacle Choir Christmas special.

But as you stroll the countryside, peering into the greenery, don't forget that interesting animals and insects are hard to find. Using basic guerrilla warfare tactics, they tend to blend into the landscape. The dunce-cap head of the treehopper nymph, for instance, isn't as dumb as it looks—to a predator, it's simply another thorn. And ice worms appear as little flecks of grass against the broad, blue glaciers of Alaska. Even the overlooked inhabitants of our own backyards—ants and worms, butterflies and beetles— are able to do the oddest things. And, yes, toads.

"I was in third grade when I first remember hearing the toads. When the sun went down they started croaking, sounding like a creaky swing set going back and forth, back and forth. I'd listen to this strange sound all night, get up in the morning, and find my dog Ralph stiff as a board." Susan St. Clair, a Seattle tailor, grew up in Dade County, Florida, during the early sixties, a time when the manicured lawns of suburbia began to encroach on the great squirmy swamplands of North Miami; when, for Sunday dinner, Mom still served pot roast and mashed potatoes while gators slid under the house to eat the family cat. Kids took bubble baths in the same water manatees swam in at Snake Creek. Dad emptied can after can of Raid in a losing war against the flying cockroach, roughly the size of a Tootsie Roll. And every year, when summer finally yawned and rolled around, the yards filled with toxic toads of the genus *Bufo marinus*. (*Bufo* means "toad" in Latin.) "They were your basic big frog, muddy brown and lumpy," St. Clair recalls. "They had been hibernating, so they were hungry. They loved Alpo."

The toads sport a matching set of venomous glands on either side of the neck. When bitten by canines protecting their food bowls, the glands explode in a milky geyser that paralyzes Rover, or Ralph, for hours. "The morning I found Ralph he was twitching and breathing, so I knew he was alive," St. Clair says. "But his legs were sticking out stiff. On the way to school, I saw three or four other stiff dogs. At school kids would just say, 'My dog is stiff.' People tried to stand them up, but they'd fall over. We'd have to take them by their tails and throw them in the bushes until the poison wore off so they wouldn't get heatstroke."

The Museum of Natural Science in Miami houses one of the largest *Bufos* in the world. Brian Mealy is in the aviary. A tightly built man with intense blue eyes, he is the curator at the museum. He leads me into the collection room, waves his hand toward the floor, and says, "Well, there's Jabba the Hutt." Wide, fat and bumpy, Jabba looks like a regular toad except that he's the size of a large cantaloupe. He's nine and a half inches long and weighs about four pounds twelve ounces, depending on whether he has recently urinated. "Those are the venomous glands," Mealy says, pointing to the two teardrop-shaped dark areas behind Jabba's eyes.

He reaches down and presses on the glands with his thumbs. Nothing. "Now, if a dog really sinks his teeth in there, the venom squirts out automatically." Used as a defense mechanism, the venom paralyzes the toad's predator, giving the *Bufo* an opportunity to escape.

Every spring, toxic toads invade south Florida; monarch butterflies show up at the very same trees in California; and brine shrimp, living relics of an ancient inland sea, hatch senselessly in the hollows of Utah's boulders. All over the country gold beetles hide beneath morning-glory leaves, keeping their remarkable secret to themselves—that at a moment's notice they can turn into ladybugs. There are even ants in Texas that plant rice, harvest it, crack it into meal, then make cakes out of it and set them in the sun to bake. Or are there?

"That's rubbish," sniffs Roy Snelling. "Where did you hear that one?" Snelling is the collections manager for the entomology section of the Natural History Museum of Los Angeles County. He's also an ant specialist—or, more precisely, a myrmecologist—which is why I called him to verify the story about the Texas baker ants.

After ridiculing the idea that ants "bake rice bread," he tells me about Southwest honey ants. "Just pop them into your mouth, holding on to the head and thorax, and eat them like grapes. They're delicious." The abdomens of honey ants, Snelling says, are filled almost to bursting with nectar. Several thousand live in each nest; Native Americans used to dig them out for a snack.

As convincing as Snelling was, I wasn't convinced. Not about the gastronomic joys of honey ants or the myth of Texas baker ants. Having read about baker ants in a book by a Texas naturalist who seemed to know his stuff, I decided to go to the source, Sanford Porter, a research associate in zoology at the University of Texas. "Good stories die hard," Porter says with a chuckle. "Those harvester ants were first reported back about 1860." The story, according to Porter, got into an encyclopedia and spread around the world. It was disproved early this century and has been disproved several times since then.

For every false story in the Wild Kingdom, there's an even more bizarre true one. Porter describes fungus-growing ants, "gardener ants" that strip trees and plants of leaves. Their common name, he says, is the leaf-cutter ant, of the genus *Atta*. Cutting circles out of leaves, they carry the remnants back to their colonies. They chop the leaves into smaller and smaller pieces and put them in a fungus garden. When the fungus digests the leaves, the ants eat the fungus. The colonies are huge, thirty feet deep and twenty feet across. More than a million ants live in one colony. "The queens are an inch long," Porter says, "making them the biggest ants in the United States."

After the baker ant ordeal, I want something easy, something that stands out like a woolly mammoth in an ant farm. "Ice worms," suggests Alaskan geologist Dennis Rogers. "They're neat. Related to earthworms, they live year-round in glaciers, probably eat algae, maybe pollen. Look," he says, "the Cordova Ice Worm

Festival is next week. Come and see for yourself."

When I call to make reservations, the Alaska Airlines clerk informs me that the airline is offering a "special Ice Worm Festival fare." Not wanting to seem frivolous, I make the mistake of telling her that I am on a serious scientific expedition. She finally stops laughing long enough to tell me that the festival is "just another Alaskan excuse for a party." She assures me I will see at least one ice worm—a mascot, some guy dressed up in an ice worm suit. "Ice worms are a myth, anyway. Just go and have a good time." Even my seatmate on the flight, a young lab technician who skis and hikes a lot, does not believe ice worms are real. "I've never seen one," she says.

I meet Rogers in Juneau. "This blizzard's a good one; visibility's shot," he says. "The Cordova flight's been canceled." No ice worms. No Ice Worm Festival. We do what any red-blooded Alaskan would do and head for the nearest bar. "So, are they real or not?" I ask miserably. "Of course they're real," Rogers replies. He reaches into his pocket and pulls out a small stoppered glass vial filled with little black things floating around in a clear liquid. "Ice worms," he says proudly. "A biologist friend got them for me."

They are skinny and about half an inch long, looking suspiciously like fish droppings at the bottom of an aquarium. The old geezer sitting next to us looks at me, then the vial, then me, then the vial, and finally says in a fine whiskey baritone, "You interested in ice worms, Missy?" He wears a sea captain's cap; his beard looks like a square-rigger. The sleeves of his plaid flannel shirt are rolled up, revealing cream-colored long johns. Faded red suspenders hold up his work jeans, and his belt buckle is a brass king salmon. He's missing a finger on his right hand and smells like new tobacco and old fish. I nod, responding to his question. He sets his beer down with great ceremony, takes a deep breath, and begins the following poem:

With shouts of stark amazement and with whoops of sheer delight,
They surged around the stranger, but the first was Deacon White.
"We welcome you," he cried aloud, "to this Great White Land.
The Arctic Brotherhood is proud to grip you by the hand. . . . "
"And now," continued Deacon White to blushing Major Brown . . .
A Sourdough is a guy who drinks an ice-worm cocktail down. . . . "
"'Tis easy done," said Deacon White, "Ho! Barman, haste and
    bring
Us forth some pickled ice worms of the vintage of last Spring."
But sadly still was Barman Bill, then sighed as one bereft:
"There's been a run on cocktails, Boss; there ain't an ice worm left.
Yet wait. . . . By gosh! it seems to me that some of extra size
Were picked and put away to show the scientific guys. . . . "
"Drink, Stranger, drink," boomed Deacon White. "Proclaim
    you're of the best,
A doughty Sourdough who has passed the Ice-Worm Cocktail
    Test."

The crowd in the bar roars its approval, and practically everyone in the place buys the captain a drink; the successful recitation of a poem by beloved Yukon poet Robert Service is a prized accomplishment in Alaska. But I'm still confused. Are ice worms real or aren't they? I need an authority, preferably not a sourdough.

"Oh, yes, they're quite real," says John Edwards, a zoology professor at the University of Washington. "I'm looking at a bottle of them from Mount Rainier right now." His bell-like British tones are wonderfully reassuring, as is the fact that he is an alpine ecologist. "I've counted as many as five hundred per square meter on Mount Rainier," he goes on. "They're about three quarters of an inch long, a dark red-brown, but they look black to the eye, particularly against the snow."

Like many other organisms, ice worms have antifreeze in their bodies, Edwards explains, so they don't freeze. "People always forget that zero degrees Celsius is not the freezing point of water; it's the melting point of ice," he says. Temperate glaciers such as the ones on the western slopes of the Pacific Northwest always have water together with ice. The ice crystals are like marbles, like lots and lots of little ball bearings frozen together with water all through. Ice worms wriggle through those marbles—actually they can move very fast. The temperature is exactly zero degrees centigrade, or thirty-two degrees Fahrenheit. There's generally a heavy snowfall before things get really cold, and snow is a superb insulator. Even though it's minus forty or fifty degrees and blowing like hell on top of the glacier, underneath that pack of snow is a very warm (thirty-two degrees F) environment.

Because the air is full of insects and organic materials including spores and bacteria, ice worms don't starve. In fact, they don't need to eat often to survive. "I've kept them in plastic bags in a cold room here for a year without any food," Edwards says, "so they can go a long time between dinners." But in order to adapt to a climate-controlled system, ice worms sacrifice flexibility. "If you warm them up too fast, everything inside speeds up so quickly they just dissolve. If the temperature drops severely, they freeze to death."

Fasting worms buried alive. Giant toxic toads that paralyze dogs. Fungus-growing ants. Where is the lyricism of nature that John Muir always wrote about? I decide it's time for an aesthetically pleasing *objet d'aventure zoologique*. Something in a plumed bird, perhaps, or better yet, a butterfly. It's early winter. The monarchs are clustering in Santa Barbara. O excellent creatures, fragile and fair. How worms and ants do pale beside your royal markings of mandarin and black. I'm on the next plane south to California.

Christopher Nagano works in the entomology section of the Natural History Museum in Los Angeles County. Officially he's a research associate, but he spends a lot of his time educating the public about the plight of the migrating monarch, a hundred million of which fly hundreds, even thousands, of miles each fall to the coastline of California or the high mountains of central Mexico, where they wait out the freezing temperatures farther north.

Monarchs east of the continental divide head for Mexico. Those west of it fly to California, weaving their way through the passes and valleys of the Rocky Mountains, then across the deserts of California. "They have to stop to fuel up with flower nectar and water on the way," Nagano says, "but the most they travel in a day is eighty miles." Like hawks, they like to ride the thermal currents because they can glide without having to flap their wings. They don't migrate in flocks, Nagano explains; they fly solo, though mountain passes often funnel them together. "They start arriving in California in September, most of them show up in October, and they begin to leave in January. By mid-March they're gone." Every year these elegant black-and-orange lepidopterans return to the same trees. Like salmon and wild geese and whales, monarchs are living metaphors for what Native Americans call the Sacred Circle, representing a worldview that respects the ongoing cyclical nature of life and is opposed to interrupting or destroying those cycles. And as usual, we're wiping them out.

"Approximately one dozen colonies in California have been destroyed or heavily damaged in the last few years because of urban or agricultural development," reports *DANAUS*, a newsletter about California monarchs named after the monarch's Latin name, *Danaus plexippus*, and edited by Nagano and colleagues

Walter H. Sakai and Gary Wolfe. Recently the International Union for the Conservation of Nature and Natural Resources made the protection of wintering monarch colonies a "top priority." The monarch is the only insect listed in the Convention for the Conservation of Migratory Species of Wild Animals—or "Bonn Convention"—an international treaty protecting many animals. And during his tenure as California governor, George Deukmejian signed into law a bill that officially recognizes wintering monarchs as a special California phenomenon. "It's the first time the state of California has admitted the environmental importance of an insect in a positive way," Nagano says.

He asks me to meet him at the Ellwood Colony at 10:00 a.m. It's a bright winter day, and following his map, I park at the dead end of a modest residential street, then venture into an adjacent grove of eucalyptus trees. It's another universe. The air is cool, perfumed with the mint and medicine breath of the gum trees. Colors are transcendent—mottled lavender and peach and jade. The ground is a crinkly mop of leaves and shredded bark that makes you want to kick at it, regardless of your age. Nagano said he'd be "in the wash with the monarchs," but everything looks the same, and I don't have the faintest idea which way to turn. I'm lost. Then, with that same bewildering otherness that imbues the whole place, a monarch butterfly appears out of nowhere and flies right past my nose like a guide manifest. I follow.

We make a sudden left-hand turn, and there is Nagano, sitting cross-legged beneath a tree with a long-handled butterfly net on his lap, writing in a notebook. A monarch is walking slowly up his sleeve. I'm stunned. The tree looks like it's strung with red Santa Fe chilies. No, I realize, it's covered with butterflies, and the butterflies are moving! This is a bona fide butterfly tree. The constant fanning of all their wings sounds like a light rain.

"There are about three thousand monarch butterflies here today," Nagano says, clearly enjoying my awe. "They are also known by the name milkweed butterfly because that's all they eat." It turns out that a chemical in milkweed both nourishes the monarchs and makes them toxic to most birds. "A bird eats a monarch once and never tries again," says Nagano. With a chuckle he adds, "Lincoln Brower, distinguished professor of zoology at the University of Florida in Gainesville, won an Esquire Dubious Achievement Award for determining how many monarchs it takes to make a blue jay vomit.

"You want to tag a monarch?" he asks. We hold the kicking butterflies in one hand, while with the other we carefully rub a bald spot in the powdery microscopic scales on the upper edges of both sides of one wing. Then we gently pinch on a rather unremarkable-looking small white sticky label printed with the words MAIL TO NAT. HIST. MUSEUM, LA, CA 90007, followed by a number like MP-L 38465. Nagano records the tag number in his notebook, then we let the butterflies go. The tag doesn't affect their ability to fly. Nagano says they don't even know the tag is there.

Once they die, with luck someone mails them to the museum and says where the insect was found. By checking the tag number, researchers know where it was tagged and how far it got. "One that was tagged in Toronto showed up in Mexico," Nagano says proudly.

During the time I spend in Santa Barbara I hear a story about a remarkable bug that changes colors, chameleonlike. I decide to look up Adrian Wenner, a natural history professor at the University of California at Santa Barbara. "Insects are not known to change colors," Wenner tells me with a wry grin. "Some lizards do. Some octopuses do. But not insects. One of my colleagues refused to believe me when I told him that the gold beetle [golden tortoise beetle, or *Metriona bicolor*] changes color. I didn't believe it myself until I saw it about ten years ago." Fortunately, Wenner has an hour between lectures and agrees to take me on a beetle hunt.

"We're looking for morning-glory plants with little holes in their leaves," he says. "That shows that the gold beetle has been there and, if we're lucky, still is." We find some morning-glory leaves with holes. "You can't disturb the beetles," Wenner explains, "or they'll drop, and you'll never find them." Then, moving his long, graceful fingers like a magician, he tucks a plastic bag beneath the plant and shakes the leaves. To my astonishment, five tiny beetles roll out, bright as polished gold. Wenner sets one in my palm, and to my further astonishment it immediately begins to glow a fluorescent turquoise, then a brilliant green, then it turns bright vermilion and manifests two black spots—as I am watching.

"It's turning into a ladybug," I cry.

"Yes, a good defense, since ladybugs are toxic to many predators," Wenner adds. He explains that the gold beetle manipulates its own blood. It actually pulls blood away from the edge of its skeleton so that its shape becomes nearly identical to that of the ladybug, which is smaller and rounder. Sure enough, I can see a lacy hem of exoskeletal beetle wing skirting the new ladybug persona.

Like the gold beetle, the octopus is a camouflage genius. It can change color and texture. But the biggest octopus on Earth, the giant Pacific octopus, which makes Washington State's Puget Sound its home, does something even stranger than blend into its underwater environment. Weighing up to 100 pounds, with an arm span of more than fifteen feet, it routinely draws its voluminous skin up into longitudinal folds forming numerous papillae. It looks like a giant mauve breast studded with nipples. The Houdini of the deep, the giant Pacific octopus slips its massive self through any hold, as long as it isn't smaller than its beak, which ranges from half an inch to two inches in diameter. That is an amazing feat, given that a 118-pounder was caught in the seventies in Hood Canal, south of Seattle. With a tip-to-tip arm stretch of twenty-two feet, the big beast made the *Guinness Book of World Records*.

Michael Kyte, a consulting marine biologist and one of the

better-known giant Pacific octopus specialists in the country, maintains that octopuses are quite intelligent and can be trained. At the Seattle Aquarium an octopus named Oliver moves from tank to tank on command. "And we had one, a big seventy-five-pound male named Thor, who'd fire-hose you if you didn't stop and pay attention to him when you passed his tank. They can even open bottles," Kyte adds, "both stoppered and screw top." While octopuses usually keep to themselves, occasionally an incident reminiscent of Jules Verne occurs.

Washington State Department of Fisheries biologist Feney Matthews and a diving partner were tagging rockfish off an artificial reef in Puget Sound when suddenly a very large octopus with about a ten-foot arm span began slithering up Matthews's arm. "It took both of us to pry it off. When we did, it started displaying to me, moving its tentacles up and down," she says. "Then it came right up to me again and started wrapping me up. We got it off me, and it started making this threatening action—swimming very fast toward me. We immediately left the bottom."

Kyte thinks an octopus becomes aggressive toward divers because, from a distance, a diver looks like an octopus. "I've had males get aggressive because they were guarding a mate or territory. They'll lay their arms over your head. Usually as soon as they touch you, they realize you're not an octopus and back off. But they can take your mask and regulator off, and at eighty feet, that can be startling."

Another unusual thing about octopuses is their sex life. With all those arms in the way, how do octopuses do it? Well, the male has one arm equipped for the job, with a groove that guides and holds his sperm packages so they can be inserted into the female. "When the male ejects a sperm package, it's the size of a pencil," Kyte says. "But once it hits the saltwater it undergoes a spermato-phoric reaction and rapidly expands in size to more than a meter in length. The male inserts his arm into the mantle cavity of the female, which assists the process with muscular contractions—sex at arm's length, if you will."

After one mating season, which lasts about five months, male and female octopuses die. The male fertilizes three or four females, and a switch in his brain turns off his appetite. He goes senile; then he starves to death. The female octopus lays about 50,000 eggs in a den that she guards for six months. During this time, she doesn't eat. By the time the eggs hatch, the female is dead. Baby octopuses are orphaned from birth.

Ancestors of the giant Pacific octopus have been on the planet for millions of years. They were hard-shelled creatures called ammonites and nautiloids, similar to today's chambered nautilus. They left beautifully preserved fossil remains. But it's anyone's guess when the octopus shed its shell, since the pliable entity we know today leaves no fossils. The oldest fossil genus on the planet, however, can be found flitting around in puddles and ditches all over the United States.

"Tadpole shrimp fossils, of the genus *Triops*, are identical to those found in Europe, which date back two hundred million years. So as far as we can tell by morphology, it's the same species," says Denton Belk, adjunct professor in the biology department at Our Lady of the Lake University in San Antonio, Texas. "This means tadpole shrimp are the oldest genus living on the planet," he adds.

Tadpole shrimp and their cousins the clam shrimp and fairy shrimp are mysteries of modern biology, like the scientific quandary of how bumblebees fly—aerodynamically they're too heavy for liftoff. They are shrimp that might have evolved from some sort of oceanic origin, but you can find them in the oddest places, like stock tanks and snowmelt ponds—even in the hollows of boulders. They got there through the feces of birds and dust storms—even the muddy feet of birds. Even stranger, their eggs don't hatch on a regular schedule. In fact, they can remain in suspended animation for decades. They even breathe weirdly: Tadpole, fairy, and clam shrimp—all of the subclass Branchiopoda, meaning "gill foot"—breathe through their legs as they swim.

Tadpole shrimp should really be called horseshoe crab shrimp because that's what they look like—in two-inch miniature. Clam shrimp look like little teeny half-inch clams, with the addition of a couple dozen legs and two pairs of antennae—one for analyzing the chemical makeup of water and one for swimming. And fairy shrimp are almost all legs. Fragile and feathery, they appear out of nowhere, which probably accounts for their name.

A brand of fairy shrimp called brine shrimp are the only commercially viable one of the group. They are, in fact, a multi-million-dollar business, "the backbone of the aquaculture industry," Belk says, used as food for tropical fish aquariums. "Maybe you've seen the ads for sea monkeys. Those are brine shrimp. They're sold as novelty items, as little pets." One-quarter cup of live shrimp goes for $1.50; eggs are about $4 for nine grams, or thirty-one ounces.

Brine shrimp are the only oddballs of the gang that have two modes of reproduction. They produce both live young and eggs. The first or second batches are born live. "You can see them in Utah's Great Salt Lake," Belk says. "From the air they look like red paint."

After the mother has birthed live young, she produces eggs, which can be "vacuum-packed like coffee," Belk says. "Just add water." This occurs because the mother secretes a sclerotized (leatherlike) protein that hardens around the embryo. "It looks like solidified foam," says Belk. "We're talking about something two-tenths to three-tenths of a millimeter in diameter." Mothers produce 50 to 100 of these at a time. Once the shell is set, the embryo is protected for years, even decades. Then the rains come or the snow melts, and if the temperature is suitable, the eggs hatch. Naturally enough, that's just what happens in rock holes and roadside ditches. Mothers of tadpole and clam shrimp perform the same feat.

But in many of the places where these shrimpettes live, rain isn't an annual occurrence. "The record for keeping any of these eggs and hatching them is about thirty years," Belk says. From an evolutionary point of view, no one really understands how these shrimp ended up in such places as Utah's Great Salt Lake. "Presumably their ancestors were from a marine environment," Belk says. "There just is no information. There aren't even any theories."

Not so with Florida's manatees. Scientists know just about everything there is to know about the manatees—from their evolutionary development, sexual behavior and physiology to their communication skills and feeding habits. These ancient, big, sweet, slow, vegetarian mammals, sometimes called sea cows, belong to the order Sirenia. Forty-five-million-year-old sirenian fossils have been found in Florida. Biologists believe that sirenians evolved from four-footed land mammals more than sixty million years ago, citing their undeveloped pelvic bones as evidence of terrestrial ancestors. Manatee bones also have been found in pre-Columbian Indian refuse mounds in southeastern Florida.

There's no creature in the United States even remotely as strange looking as the manatee, which reminds one of a cross between the Blob and a vacuum cleaner. The manatee is almost hairless, except for stiff, cactuslike whiskers around the face and sparse, fine hairs on the body. Thrown in to complete the absurd look: a beaver tail and flippers with three or four nails at the tip. Just under the finely wrinkled skin is a layer of fat deposits. A bulbous face and small, wide-set eyes give the manatee a sort of lost walrus look.

Found in freshwater, brackish and marine habitats, they're usually about 10 feet long and weigh from 800 to 2,000 pounds, though some grow to a whopping 12.7 feet and weigh in at 3,500 pounds. This makes sense, since the manatee's nearest living relative is the elephant. Though nobody knows for sure, it's thought that if left alone, manatees can live up to sixty years. The oldest one in captivity is twenty-nine.

Manatees have a prehensile mouth that folds in and out much the way an elephant's trunk does. In the wild, manatees put away up to 100 pounds of abrasive water plants a day, which explains their bizarre ability to wear away and grow back one set of teeth after another. This factor, biologists say, allowed the manatees to survive in the New World and replace the dugongs, their relatives in the Pacific. At any given time, new teeth are sprouting in the back jaw of a manatee's mouth. The new teeth move toward the front as the old teeth fall out. It's like an ongoing dental parade that lasts a lifetime. Even a dying manatee often has a new set of molars.

The social behavior of manatees fascinates biologists. They

have no natural enemies besides man, no social hierarchy, no daily set routines. Many of them will swim right up to divers to be petted. When manatees are together in groups, one manatee does not dominate the herd, although a manatee often initiates playtime. Manatees love to play. Between somersaults, head stands, tail stands and barrel rolls, they bodysurf, kiss, nuzzle, bump and chase one another. And eat. Manatees spend about five to eight hours a day feeding. The Flying Karamazov Brothers of the animal kingdom, what we're doing to them with our speedboats is unforgivable.

Of the 1,200 manatees left in the United States today, 900 are officially identified by their boat prop scars. "There's one huge cow whose tail is just spaghetti," says Cheryl Buckingham, a graduate student working with the U.S. Fish and Wildlife Service. During the summer months, Buckingham comes to the Gulf Coast town of Homosassa Springs, some eighty miles north of Tampa, to study the effects of boaters and divers on the 160 or so manatees that make the nearby Crystal River National Wildlife Refuge their winter home. The U.S. Fish and Wildlife Service staff—project leader Patrick Hagan, law enforcement officer Frank Brauszewski and biologist Larry Hartis—manage five refuges, covering eighty miles of Florida's central west coast.

"You probably won't see a manatee today," Hagan cautions. "It's late in the season, and they're pretty much dispersed." In summer manatees roam all over Florida's coastal waters, estuaries, bays and rivers. During the winter, cold temperatures drive the manatees to warm water discharges at power plants and natural warm water areas like the Crystal River refuge. But we take the boat out anyway and tour the nine islands and 33.12 acres of the refuge. Yellow-finned mullet leap out of the water all around us. We pass magnolia trees, red cedars and pickerelweed with their purple floral spears. There are pines, oaks, banana trees, sweet gums, cabbage palms and palmettos. And everywhere, just under the surface of the water, lies the spongy green countenance of hydrilla. Buckingham reaches in and grabs a handful. "This is the manatees' favorite food," she says. "And this is where they like to stay when it gets cold. There are six hundred million gallons of water in the whole system and more than one hundred springs. This one stays seventy-two degrees year-round—it's the biggest one."

We pull into a little half-moon bay marked by signs that read MANATEE SANCTUARY and IDLE SPEED. Ospreys, eagles, cormorants, pelicans, major league gators and countless jump-for-joy mullet—but no manatees. "You can always see them over at Nature World," Hagan offers kindly.

Nature World is just a short drive from the manatee refuge center in Homosassa Springs. It's a tourist attraction with the usual snack bar and tackola gift shop setup. But the main part is built over a natural spring, and it's really quite pretty. I meet Betsy Dearth. She works full-time at Nature World, "doing just about everything." We're standing in the underwater observation room while the dozen or so resident manatees float eerily above our heads. "Rosie circles a lot—she has an equilibrium problem," says Dearth. With a sad smile, she adds, "They really ask for nothing. They don't kill anything. They just want to float along—and eat." Nature World manatees consume fifty pounds of carrots, five cases of lettuce and three cases of cabbage every day.

I ask if I can feed them by hand. Despite the fact that state law forbids the public to feed protected species, Dearth agrees to bend the rules and leads me to a little clearing on the shoreline. Several large manatees come over—Hugh, Magoo, Amanda. I hold out a carrot, and Rosie surfaces, working her lips like gates in a pinball machine. Her breath smells powerfully of cabbage. "Their mouths are like a hand," Dearth says. Rosie takes the carrot, nudging my hand sweetly in the process.

Her touch disorients me. Forty-five million years, I think, compared to our meager 250,000. They were here with the first whales and the saber-toothed cats. When the mountains came barreling out of the seas, they were here. When glaciers took the land like a cold cancer, they were here. What are the pyramids held against the cellular memories of manatees? What is a Corinthian column? Even, I wonder, what is the Pythagorean theorem? And, certainly, what is a 5000 Scarab Meteor powerboat with a Triple 420-horsepower Merc V8 cutting twenty-foot rooster tails across what's left of the natural habitats of these ancient beasts?

The natural properties—the sun, the trees, the bays and rivers—that have supported life so luxuriantly for millions and millions of years on this long green peninsula are the very same ones that make Florida so attractive to *Homo sapiens*. Every day 1,000 people move to the state. Every month they launch 1,500 new pleasure boats. Only 1,200 manatees are left in Florida—the odds aren't good. At least for now the animals are still there, and there's a strong movement in the state to keep it that way.

If you ever find yourself discontented about our age, thinking that technology's homogenization has bankrupted the planet of its original eccentricities; that the presence of McDonald's in Beijing and of Whitney Houston T-shirts in Borneo has rendered the earth, once again, quite flat; then it is helpful to recall the day of the stiff dogs, to remember that each spring ice worms begin their tentative ascent through the thinning Alaskan snowpack and brine shrimp bloom in the Great Salt Lake like a colossal aquatic Matisse. The new greenery sends inaudible shrieks of joy through the colonies of Texas leaf-cutter ants, and gold beetles huddle in wonder at the sudden profusion of morning-glories. From Mexico to California, monarch butterflies prepare for their return trips north. The giant Pacific octopus slides along the bottom of Puget Sound, and gentle manatees float in Florida's waterways. For just beyond the roar of Mercs and Evinrudes, just beneath the dispassionate skins of Congoleum and Astroturf, that old natural magic is still going strong—and you don't have to float down the Amazon to find it. It's right here, snorting, flapping, wallowing and burrowing in America's own backyard.

Rhapsody in Blue

Jonah.

I was thinking about Jonah. In fact I couldn't stop thinking about Jonah, which, if you are one of several hundred human anchovies packed into the belly of a 747 jet vamoosolating through space somewhere above the Pacific Ocean, is not exactly a pleasant obsession. I tried to tune my headset to the Muzak channel so some horrible song like "Feeeeelings" would get stuck in my brain instead, but all I could get was Hawaiian music. Which made things worse. We were en route to Honolulu which my mind translated as "en croute to Honolulu" because it was still stuck on Jonah and insisting on picturing us baked into this whale of a metal pastry like a bunch of little tourist McNuggets who only *thought* they were heading for a good tan. Fine. Maybe ninety-nine percent of us were. But *this* muchacha was looking down the throat of a blind date with Muhammad Ali of the Deep Blue Sea. I was going swimming with whales the next day and this Jonah thing was getting on my nerves.

Okay, I wasn't *really* going swimming with whales, unless I had about $25,000 in loose change, which is the Hawaiian Department of Fisheries' fine for intentionally paddling around in whale territory without a permit in the merry month of February. That's when about 2,000 humpback whales show up off the island of Maui for their annual winter vacation. Like everyone else coming to Hawaii this time of year, the whales are only interested in hanging out in the sun and making a lot of whoopie, which is why it's a federal offense to bug them. This is their breeding season, their calving season too, and they've got enough problems with all the boat and plane and jet ski traffic around Maui without some ridiculous dwarfette water-nerd with terrible eyesight and silly black chicken feet snorkeling around in their bedroom.

However. Reliable fishy sources had informed me that should one get in the water *anywhere* off Maui one has a pretty good chance of hearing humpbacks *singing*. Their songs are so loud and carry so far that you could probably hear whale song from your hotel bathtub if you paid attention. It is, in fact, common to hear humpback solos from the shore.

"That ought to give all these sunstroke candidates a thrill," I thought meanly, regarding the stockyard full of tender white meat seated around me pretending to be engrossed in the dumb Demi Moore movie playing on the miniature screen about a whale's length down the aisle. From that distance Demi and her various love interests looked about as interesting as sand fleas—in fact they looked a lot *like* sand fleas—so I snubbed the movie and continued to search for a suitably sappy musical substitute for my Jonah Jones (it is a scientific fact that the cerebral stickiness of melodies is directly proportionate to their dork quotient, which explains why ninety-five percent of all Americans spend the better part of December humming "fa-la-la-la-la-la-la-la-la"). But my channel-hopping accidentally cut into the movie dialogue wherein Demi was telling the fortune of a severely buttoned-down woman who looked like the only future she could possibly use was a couple of bottles of Cuervo Gold and a night on the town with Bruce Willis.

"Ah . . . ah see ya'll singin'," Demi drawled.

"I do sing in the church choir," the woman replied prissily.

"No," Demi insisted. "I see ya'll in a nightclub."

"A psychic," I thought, not liking at all what I was thinking. "Demi Moore is a psychic talking about singing, Jonah was a prophet *and* the only person in history to be eaten by a whale AND I'M GOING SWIMMING WITH SINGING WHALES IN THE MORNING!"

"Well, it wasn't a humpback whale," Kona Joe was saying as he slowly maneuvered our boat out of Lahaina Harbor which had recently been made a humpback sanctuary. "It had to have been a sperm whale—that's the only species whose esophagus is wide enough to swallow a man. It *would* be creepy though," he agreed. "Sliding around in there with a bunch of thirty-foot squid. Yick!"

Then he glanced at my face, which probably looked a lot like Demi Moore's when she realized that the short, fat butcher she had just married was *not* the cosmically intended love-of-her-life.

"Look," Kona Joe offered sweetly, "you have a *much* greater chance of being eaten by a shark than a whale."

"Is she *still* whining?" Art Wolfe inquired sympathetically, having graciously stowed his several dozen camera bags all over the back of the boat, making falling overboard a distinct possibility. He is, of course, America's most famous *and* fearless wildlife photographer, having cut his Fujichrome teeth on wolves, bears and bellowing Alaska moose. Unfortunately, he was right. I *was* whining. I was, in fact, being a weenie. Art, as usual, was being Hans Franz.

"I'm Hans Franz and ve're going hafter vhales or I plant you six feet under!" he hollered to Kona Joe who hollered back: "Listen to me yesterday, don't remember me tomorrow!"

And we were off.

Kona Joe's Boston Whaler *Outrage* ripped along the watery corridor between Maui and Lanai, the pineapple island. The sea looked bluer than your usual maritime blue, sort of a Technicolor hybrid of Prussian blue and lapis, not turquoise but not navy either. The Christmas geometry of Maui revolved by on our left, yokes of emerald sugar cane fields girded with the island's blood-colored earth. Clouds snagged themselves on the West Maui Mountains throwing milky light all over this tropical farmland. It was hard to believe the ecological disaster sugar cane had brought to the place. The soil was trashed and the toxic run-off of pesticides alone had finally caused a weird species of algae to invade Maui's beaches.

"Whale spout, dead starboard, mates!" Art yelled in a disgraceful pirate impersonation.

There were, in fact, two. Then three. Possibly four. Whale spouts, that is, not pirates.

"Might be a heat rush," Kona Joe announced and nosed the boat in the whales' general direction. He meant that we might have happened upon several males vying for the favors of one female. It was clear that Kona Joe knew his humpback sociology.

He ought to. A native of the Big Island, Kona Joe is himself some kind of legendary itinerant underwater photographer who specializes in reef fish—God only knows where Art found him. These wildlife guys have this mystical international photographers' network whose members always know when someone important is shooting in their territory and they often show up to help out. Kona Joe had volunteered to take Art within the legal viewing range of Maui's humpbacks, which means no closer than 100 yards.

"Nah, it's just a warm rush," Kona Joe diagnosed once we'd caught up with the whales.

"What's the difference?" I asked.

"It's just mild mating fever with a little aggressive behavior—some fin slapping, a little bubble blowing, no Academy Award performances."

"You oughta be in pictures!" Art sang as his camera clicked away. Four good-sized humpbacks sort of loitered along off the boat's bow, roiling around, occasionally ramming into each other, and often fwopping each other on the head with twelve-foot pectoral fins like an ocean-going Four Stooges routine.

"That's a good-sized pod," Kona Joe said.

"I've been thinking podsitively all morning," Art replied.

Suddenly huge, blooping bubbles surfaced off the right side of the boat.

"Hang on!" Kona Joe cried. "One's going under us!"

I had already been through this in Southeast Alaska. Art and I had flown up to Glacier Bay last August to witness the northern end of the Pacific humpbacks' migration, which amounts to your basic whale feeding frenzy. Once they leave Alaska in the fall, humpbacks don't eat again until they return the following spring. We had watched in awe as they chased their breakfast around and under our boat, swimming open-mouthed while their multiple plates of baleen filtered out gallons of fresh Alaskan krill.

But here in Paradise the main social activity is beating the hell out of each other, among the male whales anyway. Battles over females are fierce and bloody. You don't want to get in their way.

Maui researchers have found only one thing that genuinely distracts humpbacks from their erotic business at hand: food songs. "It's common knowledge around here that somebody recorded the sounds whales make while feeding in Alaska," Kona Joe informed us. "Then they played it underwater here in Maui."

"What happened?" I asked.

"They got absolutely rushed by whales."

"Then what happened?"

"Well, the whales swam around them a while, then when they figured out it was a hoax, they left."

"Those scientists are lucky the whales didn't turn them into hors d'oeuvres themselves," Art spat.

"Look! A blue fin!" I yelled as a narrow, wing-shaped, turquoise pectoral suddenly slid by the boat.

"It's white," Kona Joe corrected. "The water makes it look blue."

These humpbacks were getting a little too close for comfort, just like they did in Alaska. My comfort, anyway. Art, of course, was happily burning film. He was getting some great, leviathanian leaps framed by the high-toned drama of Maui's Olowalu Valley rising visionlike in the background.

But I was there to hear whales sing, and if more than one male humpback is around, *nobody* sings. Researchers have proven that singers are almost exclusively male and almost all singing is done during mating season. And we're not talking little two-minute Top Forties riffs, either. Humpback whale song is a serious, complex and personalized art, the sonatas of the animal kingdom. The songs themselves are carefully remembered and deeply patterned musical compositions which, when played at fast-forward, are identical to bird song. And when they're played backward they sound like Harry Connick, Jr., on helium . . . oh, I'm *just* kidding.

Humpback songs have driven sailors—not to mention female whales—Looney Tunes for thousands of years. You can imagine sailing into Bermuda after about three months at sea and hearing loud, moaning trumpet-shrieks blamming through the hull of your ship in the middle of the night. I guess you *would* be intrigued. It was, in fact, the U.S. Navy that first recorded humpback songs back in the 1950s. And the first to recognize their intricate, repetitive detailing were whale researchers Katherine and Roger Payne.

"Within each population, all humpbacks share the same song," writes Katherine Payne in the March 1991 issue of *Natural History*. "[It's] a long sequence of varied sounds organized in patterns that . . . can be described as having phrases (groups of notes that are roughly the same each time they are repeated) and themes (groups of similar phrases)."

And it was biologists Katherine Payne and Linda Guinee who made the remarkable discovery that humpbacks actually use rhyme to remember their longest songs: "Analysis of the songs shows that when they contain many themes, they also include rhymelike material, phrases with similar sounding endings. . . . When songs contain few themes, we do not hear this sort of material."

She notes that each song is "constantly evolving" and that "individual whales always keep up with the current version of their population's song."

Thus, the song sung at the beginning of the humpback breeding season is not the same song sung at the end of it. Since whales stay pretty quiet when they're not breeding, one would expect these Hawaiian crooners to utterly forget last year's song during their six-month Alaskan feast. But, when they cruise back into Maui the following year, they all sing *exactly the same song they were singing at the end of last year's breeding season*.

"Singing, not silence, is what brings on change," Katherine Payne explains, "and the song changes most and fastest when the most whales are singing."

Like the living human language, humpback songs, then, are cultural invention, not Neanderthal blithering repeated over and over ad whale nauseam across the millennium. So the song you hear at any given moment will remain the same for about a week, then it's gone forever, kind of like pop music of the deep blue sea.

It was noon and the ocean had been relatively quiet.

"I think we've hit a whale-free zone," Kona Joe observed. "But keep looking—even a strange wave can look like a whale."

At that moment, like a giant, visual, double entendre, *two* humpbacks breached clean out of the water not half a mile off the bow of our boat.

"A double breach!" Art breathed. "I've *never* seen that."

"Me either," Kona Joe said. "Whoa."

Within minutes the whales breached again, one visibly smaller than the other. Either this was a humpback version of Driver's Ed. or one amorous couple was practicing for the Whale Winter Olympics. Art took his station behind his tripod which he'd set up on the boat's bow, then watched helplessly as the tandem jumpers breached a third time, this time even farther away.

"What a couple of blubberheads," Kona Joe sighed. "They jump all day, they jump all night. They almost never get it right."

"Sounds like a song," Art replied.

"A whale mating song," I added. "Speaking of songs, can we take a break from the camera thing and look for a singer?"

"Whats-a-matter, you got lens envy?" Art inquired tactfully.

An annoyed-looking flying fish launched itself out of the water and almost hit him in the teeth. Nonetheless, the Whale Gods denied my request. For the rest of the day we saw a goodly amount of whale spouts, fin flapping, tail wagging and heart-stopping breaches that finally drove Kona Joe to unsheathe his own camera and join Art on the prow of the boat. But we did not hear a single singer. Finally, Kona Joe announced that it was Snorkel Time.

"Gentlemen," he said, "lower your lenses."

"You *cannot* laugh *and* snorkel at the same time," Kona Joe called down from the boat. It was too late. The butterfly fish had tickled my face again and I was about to choke to death.

Kona Joe had motored us over to some of his favorite snorkeling water off a quiet side of the island of Lanai. Art and I had struggled into our wet suits and flippers, then dork-walked over to the boat's ladder and flapped on into the sea. I fully intended to hang onto the bottom of the ladder while I cased the place for sharks, and to my surprise, Art did too.

"I'm not a real strong swimmer," he confided, which through his snorkel sounded more like some kind of Arabic prayer. But Art had sunk a ton of money into his new underwater camera and a pair of twin headlight-like waterproof flashes. He needed tropical fish photos for a future book, and damn if he wasn't going to get them. So he bravely ventured a few feet away from the boat while I clung to it like a baby sea horse afraid to swim on my own. Finally, I forced myself to look under the water.

What I saw was glorious. A wide, brightly lit world filled with transparent turquoise water and finished with a compelling assortment of colorful ocean floor sea things, many of which looked like brains-on-drugs. I was sure those were giant clams and, being the world's worst distance estimator, privately wondered if it were possible for one to bite the tip of my flipper until I actually *looked* at my flippers and realized that they were probably a good thirty feet away from the nearest clam mouth.

That established, I released one hand and, keeping the other firmly attached to the ladder, I paddled around in, oh, I'd say, about a four centimeter diameter. At which point Kona Joe sneakily forced my other hand off the ladder by smushing crunched-up tortilla chips into it. And, Whapp-o, I was instantly attacked by several million electric yellow fishes that *came out of nowhere*. And, naturally, if *they* could be hiding right in front of your face, so could Jaws.

But I didn't have much time to consider that comforting thought because several kazillion little black fish—durgons— had suddenly shown up too, fighting viciously with the yellow fish—millet seed butterfly fish—for the stupid corn chips which were still stuffed into my fist. In desperation, I flung them in Art's direction.

"That was good!" he gargled when we both came up for air,

neither of us having quite got the hang of snorkel-breathing yet. "Throw some more about three feet in front of me."

So I did. And Art's flash flashed while dozens of fish swarmed in front of him. But enough chip crumbs had fallen in front of me to attract a small herd of my own whose kissy little mouths started nibbling *on my face* when the chips ran out. Which is when I cracked up and filled my snorkel with water again and I came sputtering out of the sea like an idiot. I tried to hoist myself into the boat but my hands slipped. They were covered with thick grease, the underwater gift of the fried tortillas.

"Yuck! I'll *never* eat nachos again!" I whaled.

Kona Joe just shrugged and said, "Fish and chips."

Over dinner that night Art confessed that the odds of his getting any halfway decent incidental underwater whale shots were about the same as Pee Wee Herman's chances of guest hosting for Billy Graham. We probably would have had a serious discussion about the situation, but our food arrived and since we happened to have blundered upon the best Thai restaurant in the known universe, neither of us said much after that, being way too busy with our fresh prawn and coconut milk soup, fresh prawns and eggplant, and rice noodles with fresh prawns.

After dinner we drove to the home of yet another photographer pal of Art's who had arranged an entire slide show of other

Maui photographers' work, all of which was very good. But the slides that stopped both Art and me cold were some fantastic underwater shots of humpback whales.

"It would take me *years* to get anything that good," Art sighed on the way back to the hotel.

When I awoke the next morning the first thing I saw was whale spout. I had chosen my hotel because guests in waterfront rooms had often reported seeing whales, but this was ridiculous. Whales were exhaling all over the place out there not even a half mile beyond my lanai. I couldn't wait to get back in the boat.

A chilly wind came up almost as soon as we got past Lahaina. The surf slapped itself onto the shore like albino pancake batter and the water crested in little butter tufts. From a distance it was hard to tell if what you were staring at was a whitecap, another boat or a breaching whale.

"This is starting to suck raw dogs," Art proclaimed delicately.

We battled the wind for about half an hour, then, in the strange way of the air and water currents off this pretty island, we entered some sort of inexplicable quiet zone.

"It's the Maui Triangle," Art pronounced. It *was* spooky.

The wind dropped to a playful zephyr, the Pacific reclaimed its name and the boat stopped beating itself up on the waves. Then we heard it. Whale song.

It rose from the sea like the gut-music of some ancient being, faint but powerful. A distant howling and moaning, pleading, bellowing, that slid up your bones and rang in your head like the weirdest wake-up call you've ever heard.

"No word conveys the eeriness of the whale song," Peter Matthiessen wrote in *Blue Meridian*, "tuned by the ages to a purity beyond refining, a sound that man should hear each morning to remind him of the morning of the world."

. . . and remind woman that she is going swimming with a monster in a couple of seconds. I knew it was coming. And I had no choice.

"If you want your story," Kona Joe yelled, "get in the water *now*."

We didn't know exactly where the whale was. We knew he was far enough away to be legal and close enough to be extremely audible—under good conditions, whale song can travel up to five miles underwater. We also knew that this fellow would be hanging upside-down somewhere below, which is the humpback's chosen singing position.

Art and I stripped down to our swimsuits while I privately lamented having eaten so many shrimp the night before. "What if we smell like krill?" I thought.

Fortunately there was no time to think. We threw on our masks, snorkels and flippers, and fell overboard. And I can tell you that your imagined fear of sharks or even whales is nothing,

nothing compared to the primal terror of a bottomless pit of empty, blue water. Chinese enamel blue. Blue glass blue. Liquid sapphire cooling steel gas flame blue. There is surely no other blue in this universe like it.

There were also no points of reference. Just the white underbelly of the boat that looked especially insignificant with all that water beneath it. There is, in fact, just you and the endless, subaquatic, Hawaiian blue nothing into which you have been foolish enough to hurl your shrinking pink body.

"Put your head under the water!" Kona Joe cried, seeing that I had already resurfaced.

I did. And the high, wild singing we had heard from the boat suddenly dropped several dozen octaves. The sea, indeed, serves as a giant echo chamber for the watery scale of whale music. Its delirious notes played my ribs like a xylophone. I felt as though I myself had become the sound and the sound was everything, a terrific confusion of the senses that allows us to slip out of our known boundaries and into that still, hot place where Einstein's indestructible energy lives. If this is the mating call of the humpback, God only knows what their matehood is like.

As abruptly as the singing started it stopped. Art and I fought for position on the bottom of the ladder.

"This is not my domain," concluded the man who gladly snaps pictures three feet from drooling grizzly bears. Through his snorkel it sounded like he was ordering Chinese food.

By the time we hauled our bodies back on board, I was shaking with fear, excitement and an overdose of undifferentiated electricity. I had heard a whale and he had, most certainly, heard me. I wondered if I had, in fact, been rhymed to.

Whatever I heard, it shall never be heard again, not that song sung that way, because whale music is a living thing created deep in the mysterious four-layered brain of the humpback whose mind has been evolving some sixty-three million years longer than our own.

Back in Lahaina it was business as usual. Overcooked tourists bought "Eat Now, Diet To-Maui" T-shirts while mutant algae creeped down the beach. But later that evening traffic backed up from one end of West Maui to the other. A mother humpback and her new baby were cruising along Lahaina Harbor, very close to shore.

I, of course, watched the whole thing from the box seats on my lanai. The mother swam as slowly as she could but the little one kept falling behind. Their twin exhalations hung in the air like question marks begging the question: Will we manage to protect these wise, old beings from the folly of our ways soon enough to learn the lessons held for us still in their ancient minds? Did the whale spit out Jonah because it disapproved of his prophecies or because *it* read *his* future and seeing a kinder, gentler possibility, decided to give us a second chance?

Birds of Praise

From the plane window the clouds looked like Maxfield Parrish frosting—persimmon edged in violet glossed with gold. Flying, these days, is indeed a piece of cake. We leave Earth nonchalantly, spend our time above the weather preoccupied with worldly things. And when we get to where we're going it is as though we never left. O, wingless species mine, the miracle of having flown hath crashed and burned within us long ago. At least I thought it had. Until I spent a day in the high desert around the Snake River Canyon in southwestern Idaho, home of the densest population of birds of prey in North America.

The place is a regular raptors' Valhalla. Falcons and eagles, hawks and owls, nest easily in the breaks and ledges of the steep canyon walls. They soar and wait in the air currents that push heavenward off the cliffs there, scouting the steppes from above for ground squirrels which burrow and proliferate in the good Pleistocene silt that mantles the earth north of the rim of the canyon. The cliffs, the wind, the rarified soil and its stocked pantry contrive a support system for birds of prey unlike any other in the world, and in an uncommon alliance of government agencies and environmentalists, Congress agreed to set aside more than 480,000 acres of the canyon and its grasslands to be called the Snake River Birds of Prey Natural Area.

All visits to Idaho's birdlands do well to begin with a tour of the World Center for Birds of Prey. Built on a hill on the south rim of the Boise Valley, the center is a triumphant bird nursery, owned and run by a twenty-seven-year-old peregrine falcon recovery program called the Peregrine Fund.

The fund was founded in 1970 at Cornell University in New York by Dr. Tom Cade. Peregrine falcons were once found everywhere in the world except Antarctica. But by 1960, the use of toxic pesticides, especially DDT, had so reduced peregrine populations that there were no known nesting pairs east of the Mississippi, and only thirty west of it. Cade and his staff decided to attempt raising peregrines in captivity for the first time. It worked. It worked so well they launched a breed and release program at Cornell. Two years later they set up the Rocky Mountain Peregrine Breeding Program in Fort Collins, Colorado, supported largely by the National Audubon Society. In the late seventies, a third program began at the University of California at Santa Cruz. Then, in 1981, the Peregrine Fund's Board of Directors approved a new global focus, and construction for the World Center for Birds of Prey began in 1984. Now, Cade himself lives just down the hill.

Since 1970, the Peregrine Fund has raised and released over 3,000 peregrine falcons into the American wild—last year, 135 were "hacked in" in the Pacific Northwest. Now, thanks to the Peregrine Fund, there are over 100 nesting pairs in the eastern states, 500 pairs in all, and the center hopes for similar success with its international species, from Madagascar's little Mauritius kestrel to the mighty Harpy eagle of Central America. And if you show up in person, you get to see them.

The center is located beyond the ranchlands southwest of Boise, which you must pronounce "Boy-CEE" not "Boy-ZEE," lest you be taken for an out-of-town dweeb. Technically, however, it should be pronounced "Bwah," or, more precisely, "Le-bwah," in honor of the original French trappers who followed the Boise River to a copse of woods and cried, "Le bois! Le bois!" But then, the Owyhee Mountains to the southwest were so named in honor of Hawaiian workers who came to work in the Idaho gold mines, despite dubiously phonetic spelling.

The Owyhees had, for the moment, vanished beneath a lowering pewter sky, and thick-furred horses stood close in their pens, pawing at the stubble holding fast in this basalt basin. When you turn onto Flying Hawk Lane and head across open country toward the center, the wind hisses at your windows. It sings through your earrings when you finally get out of the car.

But inside all is calm. Administrators minister to phones and paperwork in neat offices, and biologists stroll around deep in ornithological thought. Since I was not a group, I was left alone in the main room while my tour guide, sterling volunteer Nancy Freutel, fetched her assistant.

Through glass walls I could see row after row of egg incubators—in April and early May baby birds hatch there. In the glass display cases I could see history. There are leather bird hoods— gentle blinders with a space for the beak, a traditional tool of falconry, which is, you learn "one of the world's oldest sports/arts."

Then there is the heartbreak of DDT. Small birds ate sprayed insects, peregrine falcons ate small birds and the pesticide thinned their eggs so badly they broke under the weight of their own mothers. DDT was finally banned in the United States in 1972, and deemed fit only as a Third World export, one of the reasons, along with merciless habitat destruction, that the center has committed itself to righting the plight of raptors all over the world.

The DDT story ends with a nest of healthy peregrine falcon eggs, crimson and jubilant as Easter eggs. I was contemplating their symbolism, a resurrection of another color, when Nancy walked in with Helen, and all my thoughts dissolved in the gravity of their own abstraction.

Helen was a miracle. Helen was a vision. A two-foot celebration of form and function. And femininity. In five seconds, Helen challenged everything I thought I knew about womanhood. She was as fierce and forgiving, intense and gentle, as imperious, tolerant and exquisite as Georgia O'Keefe, Isabel Allende and Mother Teresa neatly folded into one fair-feathered form. Helen was a female peregrine falcon, and you could not look her in the eye without splicing into a warrior energy as old and sure as the planet itself.

With Helen standing patiently on her gloved left wrist, Nancy began her educational speech: Peregrines see eight times better than we do—they can spot a pigeon a mile away. They are the fastest bird on earth, and they are meat eaters, using their razor-edged talons to strike prey in midair, their hooked beaks to sheer the flesh; if their prey isn't dead when they bring it down, they sever its spinal cord with their tomial teeth, angled edges built into the sides of their beaks.

I appeared, I am sure, to be an attentive student, but the truth is these falcon facts raced past my ears and hovered in the updraft of Nancy's voice somewhere above our heads. The only fact my mind registered was the fact of Helen. That she was there. And she allowed me, a stranger, to be that close.

It was clear that the center knows exactly what it is doing. A bird of prey seen in the wild is merely a distant and dis-countable cross in the sky. But, once you have been in the presence of an animal as powerful as a living peregrine falcon, you belong to it forever more. And you will insist always that it and its kind be protected from your own species' mistakes.

It is, then, restorative to know that the World Center for Birds of Prey exists. And the program works. Hope builds upon hope when you follow Nancy from chamber to chamber in the breeding barns. There is the black and coral glory of Africa's Bateleur eagle with its extra-short snake-catching toes; the co-lossal condor, North America's largest bird, inching away, thanks to the center, from the abyss of extinction; the snowy Arctic tundra gyrfalcon; the masked aplomado falcon, former native of the Southwest and another casualty of DDT poison-ing, now being brought back with the cooperation of the Mexi-can government; rare Teita falcons from Zimbabwe—in 1989 the center hatched the first ever in captivity; the elegant and huge Harpy eagle, with charcoal wings, butter yellow talons as big as grizzly bear claws and grey and white leg feathers as designerly as Esprit bedsheets; and golden eagles, with their six- to seven-foot wingspan, the biggest raptor of the Snake River Canyon area.

"This is Gwinne, our golden eagle," Nancy said as the bird looked upside down at her red mittens. "She's the one who worked with Morely Nelson and Idaho Power to redesign power poles so eagles would stop being electrocuted. Morely lives in Boise—he's one of the reasons the center is here. Steve Gwinn works with Morley quite a bit—he leads a lot of Steve's trips."

Steve Gwinn had, in fact, arrived. He is the owner and chief tour guide for his own company, Birds of Prey Expeditions, which specializes in raptor-watching float trips down the Snake River Canyon. He had volunteered to take me there, and within minutes we were heading out across the pale landscape while the sky came closer and closer to doing a belly flop on the Snake River plain.

"This whole area used to be under a glacial lake," Steve said. "That's why the mountains are all terraced. There!" he pointed. "Those are Morley's new power poles."

They were graceful things, the conductors suspended from one side only, like bells. Older poles have been fitted with elevated perches or pole-top extensions to keep birds above the lines.

"The problem is the golden eagles' huge wingspan," Steve explained. "Morley proved to Idaho Power that eagles can land on power pole crossarms, touch two wires or transformers with their wingtips and electrocute themselves. With his designs, they can't. And that black spot, about nine power towers down, is a nesting box, another Morley experiment. Before the lines were strung here, fifteen of the twenty-two boxes were *already* being used."

Up ahead, tumbleweeds loped across the road like bear cubs, and the road itself disintegrated as we passed, flying up around the car like powdered chamois.

"That's Sonoran soil—you'll only find it on the north side of the Snake. This is ground squirrel country."

This was also, therefore, raptor country. Ravens rose and fell, cackling at the clouds as they came apart, and a prettily marked bird suddenly dropped out of the sky to our left.

"Female marsh hawk," Steve instructed. "Also called a northern harrier—you can tell by the white band across her rump. Oh, they're a beautiful bird, very light of wing. She definitely had a squirrel."

We drove down a small side road, then Steve parked the truck in an endless unfenced cow pasture. Big black cattle . . . *very* big black cattle turned and watched us step into the sagebrush.

"Those aren't bulls, are they?" I asked Steve.

"No, bulls would be in a pen . . . wouldn't they?" he replied, and heroically led us across the field. The wind blasted down the valley from the north. A rattlesnake skin clattered against the cheat grass at our feet. And then the earth fell away in front of us.

There it was. A bird's-eye view of the planet's innards. The unexpected Snake River Canyon. All you could do was stare.

The river ran down it like hot lead, digging deeper into this terra un-firma, this geo arteria, which in Latin means both artery *and* windpipe. The wind, indeed, whistled through it hard enough to etch "Amazing Grace" on the cliff walls in invisible ink. We stood speechless for minutes.

"All of this is Bureau of Land Management land," Steve said finally, motioning to the canyon and beyond. "The BLM, Idaho Fish and Game, the World Center for Birds of Prey, Idaho Power, even the ranchers—all of us pushed Congress to make this the Snake River Birds of Prey Natural Area. About 31,000 acres of it is the canyon itself. The rest won't interfere with livestock grazing or even hunting, just farming. But the economics of irrigating this land are out of the question anyway, since they'd have to pump the water up the canyon wall. . . . Hey!" Steve hollered. "Now *that's* what I wanted you to see."

A pair of prairie falcons chased each other across the cliffs in front of us—even from a distance you could make out their Pancho Villa moustache markings. They looped skyward then drilled straight down in daring aerial dives, a prelude to their annual courtship ritual.

If you could stay long enough, you would surely observe the better part of the Snake River's resident raptors: golden eagles, prairie falcons, American kestrels, a sextet of owls—great horned, long-eared, short-eared, Western screech, common barn and burrowing—and a quintet of hawks—red-tailed, ferruginous,

Swainson's, marsh and sparrow. If you timed it right, you could also see members of the migrating populace of bald eagles, peregrine falcons, ospreys, merlins (pigeon hawks) and their hawk cousins: sharp-shinned, cooper's, rough-legged and Northern goshawks, one of the Snake River's rarest visitors.

The snowstorm finally spit its first flakes into the canyon. Steve looked at his watch.

"Morely is probably flying his birds right now," he said. "We can catch him if we hurry." We trotted back among the dazed cattle under a gray silk hoopskirt of a sky.

Morlan Nelson lives on the edge of a wide ravine. Spry and lean even at age eighty-eight, he is, by anyone's guess, the most famous falconer in America, having hunted with the kings of Saudi Arabia and the erstwhile ruling family of Kuwait, and he's on a first-name basis with both Paul Newman and Robert Redford. It was Morley's birds who starred in many of Walt Disney's nature films, as well as six episodes of *Wild Kingdom*. No wonder his own profile is quite raptorlike.

Besides tending his falconry birds, Morely nurses sick or starving raptors, or, more often, those shot or hit by cars. Once they're healed they're released, unless they can't fend for themselves in the wild, like Pearl, the bald eagle whose image graces every Express Mail package.

Morley cares for them all in handmade aviaries behind his house and his patience with them and love for them is tangible.

He flies them in the ravine almost every day. We were just in time to watch Shahin, a peregrine falcon, fly for her supper.

"Come on, Big One," Morley asked her gently. "Let's go." Shahin squawked and quickly flapped onto his gloved arm. "Boy, does she want to go," he said. "You just can't believe how they are." He attached a tethering leash to leather strips—jesses— fastened around her ankles, and together they hiked up the path to the crown of the ravine.

Morley undid the leash and Shahin flew off and perched on a big tree branch while he walked downhill about a hundred yards. From a worn leather pouch attached to his game belt hung a single duck head—Shahin's reward—hundreds of pounds of them are donated by a company that dresses and cleans ducks for hunters. Morley raised the lure, a leather holster fitted with real duck wings, and swung it around his head like a lariat, then let it fly, but Shahin stayed where she was. He tried it again. Again the lure fell unscathed into the dirt.

"Come on, Big One," he coaxed. "Let's go." Morely swung the lure once more in an overhead orbit. Shahin ruffled her feathers. "She's gonna go," Morely said, and sure enough, in seconds she took off low across the sky, disappearing over a knoll. For a second I feared she had flown the coop. Then, without a sound, she came blistering back over the other side. Morely let the lure fly, and the falcon hit it like a winged Patriot missile. And I knew then why Morely says that raptors' most important gift to humanity has always been inspiration. And why Steve Gwinn says Morely is really an eagle trapped in a man's body. And why a World War II pilot clocked a peregrine falcon passing him in a dive at over 170 mph. And why on my own flight home, all I could do was listen to the wind over our wings.

Buffalo Gals

The cowboys headed out under a shelf of platinum sky. They rode easy, slow, like they were going to mend fences or check on a new calf, like they were enjoying this terra cotta day. But far across the Flathead Valley dust devils drilled the palomino earth, and a bone-dry wind came up out of nowhere.

Susan and I shut our eyes. The grit got in anyway, and stuck to the sweat rivers on our cheeks like yellow war paint. We hid our cameras under our shirts and leaned into the wooden railing.

We had passed ourselves off as photojournalists so we could get this close; that's why we were crouched in the dirt under a wedge of plywood platform at the juncture of two fences, waiting.

The others waited above. Ranch folk, mostly, lined up along the hunter green cat-walks skirting the top of a complex system of stock pens and corrals. Men and women in matching uniforms patrolled the crowd. They knew a lot of people by name, knew their children. The only difference seemed to be that they were working hard and everyone else had taken the day off. We were all there on this autumn morning to witness what was left of this continent's great dramas of man and beast, the annual roundup at the National Bison Range on the Flathead Indian Reservation in Moiese, Montana.

The 18,500-acre National Wildlife Refuge supports between 300 and 500 bison, or buffalo—the names are interchangeable. Two hundred years ago, some fifty million bison ruled the American prairie, from the Rockies east to what is now Ohio, and from what we call Texas to what is today considered northern Canada. Two thousand miles long, 600 miles wide—the richest, biggest natural grassland in the world. Until the 1840s, wild bison moved across America's brittle heartland in a great and endless circle. They wintered as far south as Mexico, summered as far north as Great Slave Lake in Canada's Northwest Territories.

Iron-rooted prairie grasses were plentiful then—rough fescue, bluebunch grass, Illinois bundleflower, Eastern gama grass, they all helped the bison build their herds into the fantastic numbers that so astonished white settlers. In 1871, U.S. Cavalry troops watched one colossal herd run through the Arkansas River Valley. The animals filled an area twenty-five miles wide and fifty miles long. It took three days for them to pass.

We all know what happened. We saw *Dances with Wolves*. The slaughter scene was done with polyurethane buffaloids, but the event itself was history, not Hollywood. In a mere forty years, from around 1840 to 1880, whites nearly annihilated the American buffalo, which were shot, stripped of their hides and tongues, and left to rot on the Great Plains like smallpox sores. By the late 1800s, only an estimated 1,000 bison remained, the majority of which were privately owned. Of the millions of wild bison that once roamed the Great Plains, less than 100 were left at the turn of the century.

As it happens when things have gone too far, a public outcry finally arose, inspired by the good work of the American Bison Society and its leader, the naturalist Dr. William T. Hornaday. President Theodore Roosevelt wrangled funds to buy and fence a buffalo preserve on Red Sleep Mountain, part of the Flathead Reservation which had been created half a century earlier.

Government issue brochures simply state that the land for the National Bison Range was "purchased from the Flathead Indians in 1908." But a visit with the Flathead Culture Committee in the nearby town of St. Ignatius produced interesting details, notably a published story by an elder named Mose Chouteh:

> I was already a young man of good knowledge when this mountain was taken away from us to be a buffalo range. It was to be fenced in and buffalo were to be in there and the Indians could hunt buffalo whenever anyone wished. . . . We were told we would be paid $8,000 and some odd dollars. The Indians didn't agree to this . . . there was a big meeting held. The Indians said, no, it was good that they could go there and get their food of whitetail and blacktail deer, blue grouse, wild chicken, ground hog. This is our place to hunt. . . . The white people said, "No, we already paid for this . . . we're just telling you that is the way it's going to be." The superintendent said, "There is no way that you could break this. It is already done."

Mose also recalled that when thousands of fence posts and barrels of paint arrived at the railroad station, destined for the new Bison Range, a "hobo rolled a smoke" and threw it lit into the dry grass there and the fence posts and barrels all burned in a great, fuming explosion.

Much later, a second delivery of posts arrived, and a large number of workers—"all white people, no Indians"—put in thirty square miles of fence, and, as Mose says, "This is where the buffalo increased on this mountain."

The American Bison Society raised $10,000 to purchase thirty-seven buffalo from the private Conrad herd in Kalispell, Montana, which wouldn't have existed at all if it weren't for Walking Coyote.

Walking Coyote was a Pend Oreille Indian, one of the original tribes of what is now western Montana. In 1873, he and a hunting party set out in pursuit of the winter's meat supply, leaving their home on the Upper Flathead River drainage basin for the plains east of the Rockies. In an act of precognitive clarity, Walking Coyote returned with four young bison calves. They spawned what became the famed Pablo–Allard herd, part of which fostered the Conrad herd and, on October 17, 1909, the core brood stock of the National Bison Range. The descendants of Walking Coyote's bison were what we had come to see.

"This your first time?" asked the pale young man standing beside us. He had been assigned this wood and dust cave earlier that day and had survived the first few cuts in which a clutch of buffalo stampede by at hoof-level a little too close for comfort.

Cutting is what wranglers do during the annual Bison Round-up. Each fall, eight to ten of them ride onto the range, cut out a small group of bison, and ride herd on 'em down to the stockyard for innoculation, branding and, in some cases, for market. The Range can only handle so many animals, so the herd size has to be controlled, which explains the Buffalo Burger signs all over western Montana.

Our stationmate had quickly become an expert on this business of almost being trampled—though, I must say, he looked more like a human scallop than a ranch hand. His face was bloodless and soft and his eyes remained fixed on a spot in midair while he talked non-stop about how scared we were going to be when the bison finally showed up—precisely the kind of guy who brings out the Thelma *and* Louise in most women. Especially my compadre, Susan Ewing, a fine Montana outdoorswoman who has skinned an elk with her bare hands. Lucky for him, the ground beneath us began to quake or else Ms. Ewing would surely have reduced Scallop Man to seafood pâté.

A cowboy whoop rose in the air above us. Then another. And another. Then all sound was swallowed whole by the primal, virile power of buffalo thunder.

"They're coming!" the Scallop Man yelled, but we didn't hear him. We rested our cameras on the bottom rail of the fence and focused on the twenty-foot tsunami of dust coming our way. We had been told to hold still because bison spook easily and could turn on the riders. We knew that from time to time they also leaned a little too hard on the fencing and smushed whatever was on the other side. We were supposed to be absolutely terrified at the prospect of a dozen thousand-pound animals hurling themselves in our general direction. But we weren't.

With primordial glee, we watched the first mammoth, woolly face emerge from the ochre cloud, its tiny eye bright with fear.

Moisture glistened in its sculpted nostrils, a perfect half-moon horn rose heavenward behind each twitching ear. Our cameras clicked like rattlesnakes.

A smaller one, a cow, ran close to its flank, several yearlings followed, then another big cow with a very disoriented brick-colored baby. Then there came a head so grand and wide it filled the visual field of our lenses. It was a male, a magnificent bull, with a hump as big as Nevada. A mantle of blond fleece framed that Herculean head, draped over his shoulders like a fighter's cape, and a dense beard swung from his chin a foot off the ground, giving him the look of a billy goat on steroids. His powerful shoulders flexed and pulled, deferring to a monumental rib cage then the sveltest of loins, the rear-view trademark of the bison. Theirs is the classic athlete's build: shoulders like the Great Divide, hips as trim as a panhandle. Witnessing him, one can readily understand Ted Turner's self-proclaimed reasons for replacing cattle with buffalo and letting them run free on his 150,000 acre Montana ranch—they *are* cuter than cows and they *do* have a lot "less fat on their rumps."

This paradisio of muscle and hide lasted all of seven seconds. Then it was the moment of reckoning when every pair of massive scapulas had to fit through the gate and into the awaiting pen at the same time. Like logging trucks in a freeway bottleneck without the benefit of disc-breaks, the bison forced their way through, instantly expanding sideways en masse. Railings wailed. Wood bulged. Bull's eye met with woman's eye and nobody blinked. We were right there with them, as close as any hunter, maybe closer. We could feel the heat of their breath, see the dirt on their hooves, smell the rich, gamey scent of them.

And there was, I don't mind saying, a kind of love there. The sort fishermen feel for their fish and hunters know in their prey. It is a love of bodies, without the sex of them, of the glory of motion as true as the movement of the earth, the elemental *going* that defines all life. And you could, kneeling there in that old dust with the great great great great grandsons and granddaughters of the original herd of American bison, you could almost feel at least a synapse of the physical deliverance their incalculable numbers once rendered.

And when you finally drive away, and the brilliant light of late afternoon sets the aspen and birch trees on fire and the Flathead Valley wind turns their leaves into strobes, you note that the place names in this country are alive too—Kicking Horse and Beaverhead, Bear Mouth and the Wolf Mountains.

If you have booked rooms, as we had that night, at a local bed and breakfast, every time you get out of your car to open yet another cattle gate, the wildness of the night will take you deeper into itself, and by the time you arrive you are not surprised by the welcoming committee of two dogs, one goat, two llamas and five scrappy kittens whose mother had been recently eaten by a great horned owl. And if it's your time, one of those little cats will claim you as its own and you will take him home and he will teach you like your childhood pets never could about the inexplicable intelligence and grace of animals and become your True North in an increasingly abstract world and you will call him, of course, Montana.

Swimming with Salmon

"What if they bite my earrings?" I asked nervously.

"You won't be wearing earrings," Eric Peterson replied. "Or anything that flashes, for that matter. But these fish are so full of eggs and sperm they can't eat anyway. They only bite if something irritates them."

Like, I thought, a couple of giant water-nerds with terrible eyesight and bizarre breathing apparatus, dog paddling around in their river uninvited. Nonetheless, for the last few weeks Eric, his brother Warren and their friends had been perfecting a new sport—swimming with salmon. Wearing wetsuits, goggles, flippers and snorkels, they would hurl their laminate bodies into the green magma of the Campbell River and bounce along its surface like human glass-bottom boats looking for fish. It was their idea of relaxation, as well as a great way to get a first-hand look at the ones that got away.

The Campbell is spawning ground for some of the mightiest chinook salmon in the province. Some weigh sixty to seventy pounds. By anyone's standards, the fish returning to the Campbell are heroes. About ten percent of all salmon eggs laid in the wild manage to escape nature's chain of harassment and grow to adulthood; one percent make it back to the river of their birth.

They meet their first enemy in utero—the wily cutthroat trout, whose lust for caviar drives it to butt its head against the bellies of female salmon, knocking their eggs right into its little gourmand mouth. Steelhead, too, are known to do this.

Then there are the birds, especially the merganser—or fish duck—the kingfisher and the great blue heron, all of which consider tiny salmon smolts a dive-worthy delicacy. These days there are humanmade obstacles as well, notably silt from poor logging practices, which smothers salmon redds—or nests. Then, farther downstream, the potent pollutants from pulp mills tend to seep into the lower reaches of the river and poison salmon fry en route to the sea.

Once the young salmon leave the river, all hell breaks loose. For the next three to five years, they travel through thousands of miles of open ocean and remain moving targets for seabirds, bigger fish, seals, otters, killer whales, commercial fishermen and, of course, sports fishermen like us. That they make it back home at all is a miracle both of navigation and tenacity, which is why the Petersons and their pals are so thrilled to swim with them. "They're the best," they told me. "The trip's fantastic. You'll love it. Just remember one thing—don't fight the river."

"The water's going to be cold at first," Eric warned. "And don't worry about sinking—you'll float like a cork."

I wasn't listening. I was too distracted by how Eric's tight wetsuit cap had pushed his cheeks forward and turned his Swedish good looks into a damn respectable impersonation of a salmon. His lips even pooched out when he spoke. "Not bad," I thought. "Maybe we'll pass."

The Campbell River is an urban river, snaking its way down the belly of the town that is its namesake. It is very green and very clear and very strong. I knelt and stuck my face into the water. Through my mask the textures of this liquid universe were magnificently magnified. Common rocks looked muscular, important. Drowned insects passed by with great purpose, trapped on the long tongue of the current. Even in these first few inches of river, the pull to the sea was enormous. Willfully subjecting one's body to the rapids before us seemed suicidal. But the guides' guidance reverbed in my ears: "Don't fight the river." I took an industrial-strength breath and plunged in.

My snorkel instantly filled with water. "Help, Eric, HELP!" I screamed, but being underwater it sounded like a series of Martian split infinitives. I tried blowing through my snorkel, but that takes air. I held my breath, what was left of it.

Nine million hours later, we floated out of the rapids and found ourselves in a deep, still pool. There, right in front of our faces, was a fish. A big, rosy, bumpy fish. It was a humpback salmon. It looked like Ronald Reagan's hair dyed red so he could slip back into the Oval Office unnoticed.

The humpie hung in the water and watched us, nose to seriously hooked nose, its tail skipping from side to side like a cat's. Then, without warning, it vanished, as if it suddenly grokked that we were neither friend nor foe but some sort of unidentified subspecies that had no business whatsoever in its river.

I admit I was secretly pleased at this reaction. Like Annie Dillard, who takes private pleasure in scaring frogs, I suddenly knew how Jaws must have felt. Or Shamu, or Godzilla, or Too Tall Jones.

Another salmon appeared. It was a mammoth chinook and it was not alone. About eight of them were traveling together. They moved like dancers, holding their ripe bodies equidistant from each other with astonishing mathematical precision.

More fish arrived. One glittery gang after another, mostly salmon, but some trout and strapping steelhead, all approaching soundlessly, then spinning Nureyev-like on their tails. But one brave male chinook decided to park his massive self in front of our faces and I thought we had a fight on our hands. He opened his mouth. His teeth looked dangerous. Our fingers, I noted, looked suspiciously like worms. Fortunately, Eric was right. These fish are interested in sex, not food, and, if anything, we looked like a Black & Decker apparition, not Salmon de Beauvoir.

So the big buck took off like the rest of his entourage, leaving scarlet and platinum trails along our peripheral vision. I stuck out a wormish pink finger and felt his slick flank flex as he passed. Through my goggles he looked like a subaquatic god, a perfect product of these waters—cold, powerful, blessed with an uncommon metallic grace, his body rouged by the heat of his mission. And I was *this close* to him. For a moment, I transcended my fear that the earth will one day suffocate beneath a modern epidermis of nonbiodegradable Baggies and gave silent thanks through my snorkel to the person who invented plastic.

So, perhaps the rumor is true: If we did come sputtering out of the sea many millions of years ago, then maybe this swimming with fishes business does gratify some saline cellular memory. I don't know. I do know that when Eric and I emerged from the river, the air felt thin and insubstantial. We moved clumsily, foreigners to our own two-leggedness. In the water we glided with the freedom of spirits, the exhilaration of flying dreams. On land we fully felt the burden of our own bodies. Gravity pulled at us like a dull ache. It was as if, in less than an hour, we too had been imprinted by the ancient forces of this old river and, like the salmon, felt obliged to return. We flapped right over to the waiting van, plopped our squishy selves into the front seat and asked the driver to take us back upriver for another round.

Where Horses Run Wild

"We're on the edge of the Black Hills here," Dayton O. Hyde announced, nodding west across the Cheyenne River to a wall of limestone buttes. "East of here are 200 miles of true short grass prairie." His gaze followed the arc from mountain to range where something new caught his eye. "Wild horses!" he hollered. "There's a herd movin' across. Let's go after 'em!"

Hyde's old pickup jerked over the rocky trails that pass for roads in this part of the West, and soon we were in the company of seven bay mares. Then there were fifty. Bays, grays, blacks, whites, chestnuts, pintos, palominos—all glossy, muscular, spirited and free. A thrilling, galloping mosaic of prairie colors filing across the plains like they owned the place.

Actually, they do, thanks to the heroic efforts of Mr. Hyde, a legendary Oregon author and rancher, and George Michaelson, the late governor of South Dakota. When Michaelson heard that Hyde was looking for land on which to establish a wild horse sanctuary, he contacted him and had him flown over to the southwest corner of the state. Hyde picked his land from the sky, then worked like hell to raise the money to buy it, and in 1988, 11,000 acres of classic South Dakota prairie became the Institute of Range and the American Mustang—IRAM for short—a remote sanctuary for some 300 wild horses that would otherwise be condemned to miserable deaths in U.S. government feedlots.

The first wild horse sanctuary was established by the Bureau of Land Management in 1968 on 30,000 acres of rugged public land near the Pryor Mountains of south central Montana. Some 140 horses still run free there, and the Pryor Mountain adopt-a-horse program is so successful that managers have more demand than they have horses.

A decade later, Jim and Dianne Clapp founded The Wild Horse Sanctuary in Alturas, California, which they moved in 1983 to a 5,000-acre site east of Redding near Mount Lassen. The sanctuary is home to 300 horses, and the Clapps offer a Sponsor-a-Horse program and adopt out between twenty and thirty horses each year.

But these valiant efforts do not begin to provide for the estimated 64,000 feral horses that still inhabit the American West. Wild horses, or mustang, have always been part of the western landscape. North America is, in fact, the animal's ancestral home. Almost any fossil site on the continent between fifty-five and twenty-five million years old can produce bones and teeth from several species of horses; fifteen-million-year-old sites can produce up to a dozen. It was there in the Miocene epoch, during the heyday of horse diversification, that horses began to graze the American grasslands which were, themselves, expanding.

Dramatic climate changes and the arrival of humans during the last million years helped drive the horse's sole descendant—the genus *Equus*—to extinction in the northern hemisphere. Fortunately, many of them had already migrated to the Old World via the Bering land bridge two million years earlier, and had managed to survive there. So, it was a homecoming of sorts when the horse reappeared in the late 1400s with the 1,500 Spanish colonists who accompanied Columbus on his second voyage to the New World.

Perhaps a few of America's contemporary wild horses could lay claim to those original Spanish bloodlines. But most are simply descendants of old ranch stock that was turned out to pasture one fall and never found again.

Left alone, mustang populations are controlled naturally, albeit brutally, by starvation. Horses are powerful grazers, they're hard on the land, and they require about twenty acres of typical western grassland each month to survive. To protect private cattle range, both ranchers and government officials are known to have surplus wild horses shot and "canned," that is rendered into dog food.

However, when the Wild Horse and Burro Act of 1971 obliged the U.S. Government to provide for its feral stock, thousands of mustang were rounded up and transferred to feedlots. And in 1976, the Bureau of Land Management launched their wild horse adoption program.

"Several thousand of the youngest and best-looking horses do go to good homes through the adoption program," Dayton Hyde explained. "But the rest . . . well, even in feedlots with proper nutrition, the mustang no one wants often become listless or sick. Some of them give up eating and die. When I saw it happen with my own eyes I stewed about it for weeks."

That was in 1988. And that was the year that Hyde decided to somehow give the "unadoptable" American mustang a place to run free. Five years and countless gallons of sweat-equity later, his dream had come true: He had the horses, he had the land and he had the place all set up for the ecologically minded tourist who liked the idea of spending money to sleep in a tepee, eat from a chuck wagon and thrill to the sight and sound of hundreds of wild mustang gleefully galloping across one of the last great pieces of American prairie, which happens to be located just twenty miles from Mount Rushmore.

A nature writer by training, a rancher by trade, at age seventy-four Dayton O. Hyde is a legendary figure in the West. The author of a dozen books, he's best known for his 1986 classic, *Don Coyote*, the story of the friendship that grew between himself and a coyote that lived on the Oregon cattle ranch Hyde had inherited from his uncle. It was there that he witnessed his first mustang.

"In 1938, when I was fifteen, my uncle sent me a letter telling me that his crew had just captured a band of wild horses," he recalled. "That was nothing to tell a boy if you didn't expect to find him on the next train."

Six weeks later Hyde ran away from home in northern Michigan and headed directly for his uncle's place. His parents let him stay. Ranch life suited him and he flourished. He helped his uncle run their 6,000 head of white face cattle, and soon he developed a particular interest in the mustang that ranged freely beyond the ranch.

"When the snow was deep, we'd go out with a load of hay and dump it for them," Hyde recalls. "But when the government began eliminating natural predators from the West—wolves and cougars—wild horses started to overbreed. I remember riding into a canyon and discovering forty wild horses that had starved to death during the winter. They'd eaten each other's manes and tails off."

It was the intimacy of those memories that moved Hyde to action half a century later when he saw hundreds of wild horses jammed into small feedlots while driving across Nevada to deliver a lecture to a conservation group there. He soon learned that most of the feral horses in the United States are stashed on government land in Wyoming and Nevada. It was Hyde's inordinate love of natural things that drove him to create IRAM, a love that is evident soon after you meet him.

"We're having a great lilac season," he had noted when we left the outer limits of Rapid City and began our two and a half hour drive to the sanctuary. Indeed, almost every home was graced with a ten-foot thick-trunked tree exploding with lavender blossoms. I had never been to South Dakota before and had assumed it was one of those brittle mineral landscapes filled with rye grass and rattlers.

"Usually it *is* buckskin," Hyde had confirmed, "but we've had so much rain. It looked like this all summer last year, too. It's plum tropical."

His gaze caressed the land as he drove, a lover's look that belied the rutted rancher's face beneath it, and the beat-up rodeo-rider's body beneath that. Standing six foot six, Hyde reminds you of a slim, brown-eyed John Wayne. But as an author, he's renowned for his lyrical treatment of natural subjects, his almost telepathic understanding of wild things. *Don Coyote* is, in fact, widely hailed as the work of a leading environmental artist, and it is Hyde's artist's eye that recognizes the irreplaceable value of nature.

"As a child, I thought I was invisible," he explains. "Wild animals were not afraid of me. I'd walk around the woods with a wild partridge on my shoulder—they would flee from my brothers."

Despite these gallant admissions, I was not prepared for the mystical beauty of the land Hyde had secured for his horses. It was as if the air were purer there, the colors brighter, and the place virtually vibrated with some kind of holy ancient energy that seemed to rise from the two and a half billion year old rock.

"When I first saw the cattle here they had such a bloom to them I knew the feed must be good. Then I came to realize that saving this land is as important as saving the horses."

Clearly, it is. The Cheyenne River runs in four directions there, that is, it makes two inexplicable hairpin turns that take it east, south, west and north in one brief stretch. The place was, according to Hyde, sacred to the Sioux, Lakota and Dakota tribes. Mountain bluebirds stitched the air as we passed there. Meadowlarks sang at us from rocks. A flock of white river pelicans streaked across the old Cheyenne as we pulled up to the original homestead that doubles as the sanctuary's office, camp kitchen and bath house. Nearby were the (domesticated) horse stables where a cowboy and two cowgirls were putting up a fence—IRAM staffers ride the property to conduct maintenance duties, but horseback riding is not available to guests. And there, on a flat far beyond the corrals, looking for all the world like a Sioux village, were the tepees, designed with faithful authenticity. On average, eight guests stay there at a time, though the sanctuary's lovely camping spots can readily accommodate thirty.

I could hardly wait to settle in, but I didn't have much of a chance to before Hyde drew me off on another hike—he wanted to use the remains of the daylight to ford the Cheyenne and look for cougars. And so we went, hiking up the red cliffs on the far side of the river, following streambeds past a 14,000-year-old Indian flint mine, walking the ridges and going rock to rock, lighting, finally, on a boulder the color of cinnabar and plum. The cougars remained elusive, so Hyde planted us where, at least, they could have been, folding up his six-foot-six, rodeo-racked body into a child's sitting position. The white freshwater pelicans obliged us with a command performance, and we sat for the longest time watching the light change from pink to copper and, finally, to soot.

That night, sheet lightning moved across the sky above the tepees like a closing curtain and rain literally threw itself on the ground. We watched the show from the safety of the homestead office with a delight that paled only when one of IRAM's volunteer cowgirls—an environmental studies student from Maine named Audrey—made a heroic dash to the paddock to move one of Hyde's prize black draft horses to its stable.

"The place always attracts young people like Audrey," he said. "They've got so much to give."

The storm ended like it began, fast and true, and I finally turned in to my tepee. In the subtle light of a Coleman lamp its interior was a welcoming sight. Warm, dry, decorated with a cow skull and wild flowers, it even had two ingenious chairs—shoulder-wide skeins of willow switches lashed into a bendable plane that attached at the top to the tepee liner and lay for a foot or so along the ground. You simply sat down and leaned back with full, fluid support.

Morning brought another hike during which Hyde proceeded to name every plant, bird and animal in sight and out.

Lupin. Yucca. Prickly pear. Skunk bush.

"And that's phlox . . . no, what is that? Oh, yes, it's sorbus berry or sugar plum. That's pine there along the river. And, oh my gosh! Look at that! That's penstemon. And look at those primroses. They're like snow! That's the prairie—it never does anything halfway."

White-tailed deer. Bobcat. Elk. Pronghorn. Cougar. They all share the land with the horses.

I asked Hyde if natural predators were a problem for the mustang.

"We don't lose any to predation," he replied. "These wild horses are pretty alert and in great condition. The only way a predator could get one is to find one weakened by winter. Some of our horses are getting old," Hyde confessed. "And we're getting a natural death loss from them. It's interesting to watch. The younger horses pick on the older ones and drive them off. When they're ready to die they just stop eating so they go into hypothermia and die very quickly and peacefully."

The most effective form of population control at IRAM is the fact that all the horses there are mares.

"The government has a surplus of wild horses," Hyde explained. "So they didn't want any breeding here."

"In five years, we've never lost one from sickness," Dayton reports. "We've never had to touch a hoof. I've got 300 now. I could handle about 500."

But would more horses harm the delicate balance of the South Dakota prairie?

"No," Hyde assured me. "Because we graze them the way the buffalo graze. We utilize the feed then don't come back to that land for a year or more until it's gone to seed again. It's a form of rotation—holistic grazing is what we're doing. These wild horses are bringing the native grasses back better than they were before!"

There is much debate, these days, about the definition of wildness as applied to horses. Suffice to say, the history of the truly "wild" horse is so obtuse that experts assure us we'll never know the whole story. It *is* known that the species *Equus przewalskii* ("shev-all-ski") is, in fact, not simply a wild version of a domestic horse, "but different, as a wolf is different from a feral dog," writes Lucy Rees in the May 1993 issue of *BBC Wildlife*. Some 1,200 Przewalski's horses, she says, are held in various zoos around the world.

So are Hyde's wild horses wild? Well, they're not Przewalskis, but when allowed to run free they clearly go back to a happier, healthier animal that re-learns how to take care of itself in the wild.

"Horses revert back to type in a few generations," confirmed Professor Jack Taylor. "They get broom-tailed and heavy-legged, big-headed. What survives is a little rugged horse."

Supper that afternoon was 100 percent authentic chuck-wagon—fresh Dakota ear corn, steaks and salad. Hyde had the big Belgians hitched to his new, black, awning-covered metal wagon, and we lumbered slowly up the Cheyenne to a picnic table set up against a rock wall. Kingfishers darted around while supper cooked and a fish leapt clear out of the water.

"I don't know what that was," Hyde said, frowning. "A wall-eye or a carp." Then he leaned back and surveyed the piece of earth around him.

"I feel that it likes me," he said. "I feel a friendship with this land. When Governor Michaelson offered it to me, I begged, borrowed and would have stolen to get it. Did a lot of begging," he laughed. "And it's a good thing I did because it was going to go to the Honeywell Corporation as a weapons testing site. Can you imagine?"

I could not.

Later that evening we took another drive up to the ridge to look for the horses. A bluebird hovered over a yucca plant as we lurched along. Then a strange, sad sound moaned in the air.

"Wind music," Dayton explained. "It's a common phenomenon on the prairie. And—listen—the distant nickering of the horses."

Sure enough, there they were, thundering up over the prairie as if on cue. And there were all the classic mustang traits—the coarse heads, the foreshortened, compact bodies so critical to winter survival on the plains. Their flanks gleamed. Their muscles flexed. Their manes rose and fell in time to the rhythmic chant of their hooves. It was clear that these horses ran for the unanswerable joy of running, for the going, not the getting there. Sure in their movement, held back by nothing, they were, there is no doubt, as glorious an expression of wildness as exists on this domesticated continent.

Hyde smiled. And sighed, and nodded, and said: "Earth hath not anything to show more fair."

About the Author

Jessica Maxwell, formerly a columnist for *Audubon* magazine, writes regularly for *Esquire*, *Natural History*, *Forbes* and *Sports Afield*. She is a contributor to *A Different Angle: Fly Fishing Stories by Women* (Seal Press, 1995) and is the author of *I Don't Know Why I Swallowed the Fly: My Fly Fishing Rookie Season* (Sasquatch Books, 1997). She lives on Oregon's McKenzie River.

The following essays originally appeared in the following publications: "The Panic Principle" in *Pacific Northwest* (June 1991); "The Ritual of Winter Steelhead" as "Catcher on the Fly" in *Pacific Northwest* (January 1991); "God Dogs" in *Pacific Northwest* (March 1992); "The Tyee Club" in *Head/Waters: A Left Bank Book*, edited by Linny Stovall (Blue Heron, 1994); "River Music" in the 1995 O.A.R.S. catalog; "Into the Mystic" in *Islands* (August 1984); "Twelve Flew into the Cuckoo's Nest" in *A Different Angle: Fly Fishing Stories by Women*, edited by Holly Morris (Seal Press, 1995); "La Serenissima" in *Islands* (June 1984); "Day of the Stiff Dogs" in *Omni* (September 1988); "Rhapsody in Blue" in *TDC* magazine (May 1992); "Birds of Praise" in *Pacific Northwest* (April 1991); "Swimming with Salmon" in *Pacific Northwest* (August/September 1991); and "Where Horses Run Wild" in *Travel and Leisure* (August 1994).

Adventura is a popular line of books from Seal Press that celebrates the achievements and experiences of women adventurers, athletes, travelers and naturalists. Please peruse the list of books below—and discover the spirit of adventure.

SOLO: *On Her Own Adventure*, edited by Susan Fox Rogers. $12.95, 1-878067-74-5. Day hiking, bodyboarding, bike riding and road tripping . . . In this collection twenty-three women share the challenges and rewards of going it alone.

ANOTHER WILDERNESS: *Notes from the New Outdoorswoman*, edited by Susan Fox Rogers. $16.00, 1-878067-30-3. Whether backcountry snowboarding or circumnavigating Lake Superior by sea kayak, the women in this book cut loose from daily expectations and push past fear to embrace both the thrills and tranquility of the outdoors.

ALL THE POWERFUL INVISIBLE THINGS: *A Sportswoman's Notebook*, by Gretchen Legler. $12.95, 1-878067-69-9. A beautifully written memoir of self-discovery and an eloquent chronicle of outdoor life.

SEASON OF ADVENTURE: *Traveling Tales and Outdoor Journeys of Women Over 50,* edited by Jean Gould. $15.95, 1-878067-81-8. Grabbing their backpacks, passports and a lifetime of experience, the women in this collection prove once and for all that the spirit of adventure does not wane with age.

A DIFFERENT ANGLE: *Fly Fishing Stories by Women*, edited by Holly Morris. $22.95, cloth, 1-878067-63-X. A new look at fly fishing through the eyes of seventeen contemporary women anglers—from Pulitzer prize-winning author E. Annie Proulx to fly casting champion Joan Salvato Wulff.

UNCOMMON WATERS: *Women Write About Fishing*, edited by Holly Morris. $14.95, 1-878067-10-9. A wonderful anthology that captures the bracing adventure and meditative moments of fishing in the words of thirty-four women anglers—from finessing trout and salmon in the Pacific Northwest to chasing bass and catfish in the Deep South.

RIVERS RUNNING FREE: *A Century of Women's Canoeing Adventures*, edited by Judith Niemi and Barbara Wieser. $16.95, 1-878067-90-7. Whether they embark on backcountry wilderness expeditions or leisurely canoeing trips, these women eloquently record the personal boundaries canoeing has inspired them to explore and push beyond.

THE CURVE OF TIME by M. Wylie Blanchet. $12.95, 1-878067-27-3. The fascinating true adventure story of a woman who packed her five children onto a twenty-five-foot boat and explored the coastal waters of the Pacific Northwest summer after summer in the late 1920s.

LEADING OUT: *Women Climbers Reaching for the Top*, edited by Rachel da Silva. $16.95, 1-878067-20-6. Packed with riveting accounts of high peak ascents and fascinating narratives by some of the world's top climbers.

WATER'S EDGE: *Women Who Push the Limits in Rowing, Kayaking and Canoeing* by Linda Lewis. $14.95, 1-878067-18-4. An inspiring book that takes us inside the world of competitive rowing, kayaking and wilderness canoeing through ten candid profiles.

Ordering Information: If you are unable to obtain a Seal Press title from a bookstore, please order from us directly. Checks, MasterCard and Visa accepted. Enclose payment with your order and 16.5% of the book total for shipping and handling. Washington residents should add 8.6% sales tax. Send to: Orders Dept., Seal Press, 3131 Western Avenue, Suite 410, Seattle, Washington 98121. (800) 754-0271 orders only; (206) 283-7844 phone; (206) 285-9410 fax; sealprss@scn.org. Visit our website at www.sealpress.com.